Adrian Peterson

FOOTBALL SUPERSTARS

Tiki Barber	Joe Montana
Tom Brady	Walter Payton
Reggie Bush	Adrian Peterson
John Elway	Jerry Rice
Brett Favre	Ben Roethlisberger
Eli Manning	Tony Romo
Peyton Manning	Barry Sanders
Dan Marino	LaDainian Tomlinson
Donovan McNabb	Brian Urlacher

FOOTBALL ● SUPERSTARS

Adrian Peterson

Clifford W. Mills

CHELSEA HOUSE
An Infobase Learning Company

ADRIAN PETERSON

Chelsea House
An imprint of Infobase Learning
132 West 31st Street
New York, NY 10001

Library of Congress Cataloging-in-Publication Data
Mills, Clifford W.
  Adrian Peterson / by Clifford W. Mills.
  p. cm. — (Football superstars)
  Includes bibliographical references and index.
  ISBN 978-1-60413-755-2 (hardcover)
  1. Peterson, Adrian—Juvenile literature. 2. Football players—United States—Biography—Juvenile literature. 3. Running backs (Football)—United States—Biography—Juvenile literature. 4. Minnesota Vikings (Football team)—Juvenile literature. I. Title.
  GV939.P477M55 2012
  796.332092—dc22
  [B]
    2011004491

Chelsea House books are available at special discounts when purchased in bulk quantities for businesses, associations, institutions, or sales promotions. Please call our Special Sales Department in New York at (212) 967-8800 or (800) 322-8755.

You can find Chelsea House on the World Wide Web at http://www.infobaselearning.com

Text design by Erik Lindstrom
Cover design by Ben Peterson and Keith Trego
Composition by EJB Publishing Services
Cover printed by Bang Printing, Brainerd, Minn.
Book printed and bound by Bang Printing, Brainerd, Minn.
Date printed: October 2011
Printed in the United States of America

10 9 8 7 6 5 4 3 2 1

This book is printed on acid-free paper.

All links and Web addresses were checked and verified to be correct at the time of publication. Because of the dynamic nature of the Web, some addresses and links may have changed since publication and may no longer be valid.

CONTENTS

1 Taking Charge: November 9, 2008   7

2 Running All Day in Palestine, Texas   16

3 The Oklahoma Years   33

4 Becoming a Feared Viking   50

5 Leading the League   69

6 He Is Legend   84

Statistics   99

Chronology and Timeline   100

Glossary   104

Bibliography   109

Further Reading   112

Picture Credits   113

Index   114

About the Author   120

Taking Charge:
November 9, 2008

The football rivalry between Wisconsin and Minnesota is like a long-running blood feud. Each state's major university competes hard every year for a large trophy known as Paul Bunyan's Axe, named after the mythical giant lumberjack. The players on the winning team get to hold the red axe head with a long wooden handle high above their heads as they take a victory lap around the field. In the National Football League (NFL), the two states' teams, the Green Bay Packers and the Minnesota Vikings, play a mini-Super Bowl twice each year in an attempt to capture the title of the National Football Conference (NFC) North division. Those games can create legends almost as large as Paul Bunyan.

The Packer-Viking game on November 9, 2008, was more important than most in this long rivalry. The winner had a much better chance of going to the NFL play-offs than the loser. And the play-offs are the road to the Super Bowl, the game all players and their fans dream about reaching. The quest for a Super Bowl ring is a heroic journey, but every quest has challenges and obstacles. The winner of this game would pass a major test.

The Packers had won the previous five games against the Vikings. If Minnesota had a chance of overcoming its rival, a second-year player named Adrian Peterson would have to take charge and carry his team. But he had never played in a game as important as this one. Many wondered how he would handle the pressure.

Peterson had burst onto the NFL scene as a rookie and set the all-time single-game rushing record against the San Diego Chargers on November 4, 2007. Twice he had run for more than 200 yards in a game, something no first-year player had ever done. But late in his rookie season and early in his second year, injuries had slowed Peterson down and opponents were designing defenses to stop him. He was a marked man.

NFL coaches and players study an enormous amount of game film and quickly adjust to change. Peterson had been a big change, and other teams were adapting to him. For example, the Packers would surely "pack the box"—putting eight or nine men near the line of scrimmage to contain his bursts of speed.

THE LEGEND OF "A.D."

The NFL and its fans were getting to know more about this new star. Peterson's childhood nickname was "A.D.," which stood for "All Day" because he could run all day. He always had energy to burn and was always in motion. The nickname, given to him by his father, has stayed with him.

Great runners in football are often either very fast or very strong. Fast players are elusive and hard to grab. Strong players can overpower tacklers and bull their way for short yardage. Remarkably, Peterson is both. He is also both quick and fast.

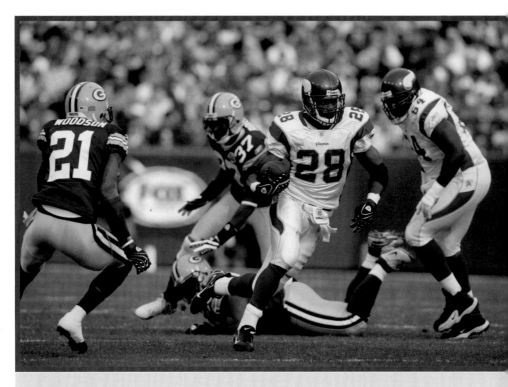

Called "A.D." by his father because young Adrian could run "all day," the nickname stuck and is still used today. The fleet-footed running back holds several NFL records, including most yards rushing in a single game (296).

Quickness and speed are different. Quickness is the ability to change direction. Speed is straight-line running.

So, like a rocket, Peterson has a boost phase and a cruise phase. His boost phase, when he accelerates, is explosive. His cruise phase, when he is at top speed, makes him hard to catch from behind. If he could accelerate for 10 seconds at the rate he accelerates for the first two seconds, he would be going faster than the speed of sound.

This Superman, though, had his kryptonite, a major weakness: He was impatient. He often did not wait for his blockers to push defenders out of the way. The Viking coaches were trying to help him control his power and wait for the blocks to develop. They had shown him game film of opposing players waiting for him to "cut back" and reverse direction to try to find open spaces and make big runs. A patient runner tends to "cut up" and will go in the direction the play is designed for, even if it means gaining fewer yards. Peterson was trying hard to change and be patient, but it wasn't natural for him. His talent needed to be developed.

Peterson had his own kind of personal rocket fuel—sadness and anger. When he was young, he watched his beloved older brother get killed by a drunken driver. A few years later, his father was sent to jail for crimes related to dealing drugs. Steel bars and Plexiglas windows separated the two for all of Peterson's teenage years. Then his stepbrother was murdered the day before Peterson had a major NFL tryout. Only his own drive, the love and protection of his parents and stepfather, and the support and encouragement of several coaches had allowed him to rise out of despair. He had endured and reached one of his life goals: to play in the NFL.

Peterson, though, was competitive as much as he was angry or sad. And the Packers would now ignite the fire that burned in him.

MAKING NOISE IN THE METRODOME

On that cold November day in 2008, more than 63,000 Packer and Viking fans streamed into the Vikings' "home dome"—the Hubert H. Humphrey Metrodome in downtown Minneapolis, Minnesota. Because the stadium is not far from the Wisconsin border, Packer fans are always well represented. Each side liked to poke a little fun at the other.

One fan wore a T-shirt that read, "I root for the Vikings and anyone who plays Green Bay." Signs with "Go Home Cheeseheads" (the Packer fan nickname) were displayed near Packer fans who wore headgear that looked like triangles of cheese. Some Viking fans were dressed in fur pelts, and many wore "Helga hats," purple helmets with white horns and blond braids attached. Official mascot Viktor the Viking wore a No. 1 jersey and a helmet with horns. As at many NFL games, there was more than a touch of Halloween in the stands. It was carnival time. And it was loud.

The Metrodome is famous for its sound. The fiberglass fabric roof helps trap any noise and make it reverberate throughout the dome. The "reverb" can be a home-field advantage: Opposing teams have complained that the ear-splitting indoor sound system gets cranked up when they are running plays and turned down when the Vikings' offense is on the field. And the Viking Gjallarhorn gets everyone's attention with its long and low battle cry. Writers in the glass-enclosed press box say that all the sonic booms make their computers vibrate and jar pieces of the ceiling loose. They feel as if they are at a hockey game when fans slap the glass windows.

TAKING OVER THE GAME

Most Viking-Packer games are hard-fought and close, and this was no exception. The teams traded touchdowns in the first quarter. The Vikings took the lead by halftime, but the Packers exploded in the third quarter, intercepting a Gus Frerotte pass and returning it for a touchdown and then returning a punt for another score. Peterson had run well but had not scored. He had not taken over the game. With less than six minutes remaining, the Packers led 27-21. The Vikings had the ball at their 31-yard line. For their offense, it was time to see how far Peterson could carry them.

During the next six plays, Peterson ran or caught the ball five times, taking his team to the Packer 29-yard line. Time was running out, though. Then, Peterson took a handoff from Frerotte and tried to find room to run between right guard Anthony Herrera and right tackle Ryan Cook. A running back's job description is to gain yards by probing for cracks in vast defensive walls, using his line as a battering ram. Suddenly, a hole opened up and Peterson's boost phase kicked in. He

THE GREATEST RIVALRIES OF SPORTS

The greatest sports rivalries are often rooted in two teams being close to each other in both geography and talent. So, many are a kind of border-war-among-equals, like the Vikings-Packers games. Other traditional pro football feuds include the Giants-Eagles, Patriots-Jets, Cowboys-Redskins, Browns-Bengals, and Steelers-anybody.

Baseball has the bitter Red Sox-Yankees and Giants-Dodgers rivalries. College football has Michigan-Ohio State, Florida-Georgia, University of Southern California-Notre Dame, Alabama-Auburn, and the Red River Showdown: Texas-Oklahoma. Hockey has the Montreal Canadiens and the Toronto Maple Leafs. NASCAR has Chevrolet versus Ford. College basketball has Duke pitted against the University of North Carolina. Pro basketball defies the geography rule by having teams at opposite ends of the country—the Boston Celtics and the Los Angeles Lakers—at each other's throats.

The most intense rivalries in sports, however, may be found in other countries. Venezuela comes to a stop when the Magallanes Navegantes (Navigators) play the Caracas Leones (Lions) in baseball. National police armed with machine guns are sometimes needed on the field. When Real Madrid plays FC Barcelona in soccer, the game is called "El Clásico" (The Classic) and is watched by hundreds of millions in several countries.

And when India played Pakistan in cricket in 1999, passions ran so high that the Calcutta stadium had to be emptied and the game resumed in front of TV cameras only. The losers in the matches between India and Pakistan are often treated as criminals by their own fans. The countries have fought three wars, and their leaders are now trying to reduce tensions. Cricket is part of a diplomatic strategy to lessen the chance for a fourth war.

shot through the space, pivoted on his right foot, and sprinted toward the end zone. One man was left to stop him, Packer safety Atari Bigby. Peterson dragged Bigby almost five yards as he lunged into the end zone for the winning touchdown. The Metrodome flash cannons roared. The reverb circled the crowd. Peterson ripped off his helmet and celebrated with his teammates. He had willed his team to victory, 28-27. He would later tell *Sporting News* writer Steve Greenberg, "That was something I'll always remember. I was in the zone."

The celebration was sweeter because it wiped out a big mistake Peterson had made on the series before the winning score. The ball was then in Viking territory with a fourth down and one yard to go for a first down. Peterson had felt so strongly that he needed to be given the ball that he yelled to his sideline to send back the punting team. "Go for it, go for it," he yelled. Fox television cameras caught the action. Coach Brad Childress changed the play and gave Peterson the ball on fourth down. The play was called "Fox 3 run," and Peterson hit a hole, bounced to another one when it closed, and was trying to break one last tackle for a big play when a Packer defender punched the ball out of his hands. Now, a running back's job description also includes not losing the ball. Fumbles—turnovers—kill drives. The Vikings recovered but came up short of a first down, and the Packers took over in Viking territory. So before Peterson won the game, he had almost lost it.

His teammates were surprised that he had become so vocal. In his roughly 25 games in the NFL, he had let his actions speak for him. Peterson is naturally soft-spoken, mature, and considerate, so urging his coaches to give him the ball was out of character. Yet he had felt it was time to step up and become a more visible leader. He told the Associated Press's Jon Krawczynski, "I am getting more vocal, and there's nothing wrong with that because you've got guys that listen."

Minneapolis Star Tribune writer Judd Zulgad follows Peterson closely. During the week after the game, he wrote:

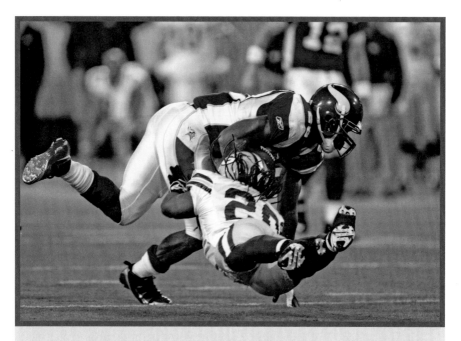

Elite running back Adrian Peterson took the NFL by storm from his very first game during his rookie season with the Minnesota Vikings. In the photo above, the often unstoppable Peterson is tackled after a carry by Green Bay Packers linebacker safety Atari Bigby (20).

If Peterson's 200-plus-yard outings in 2007 are to be remembered as the games that established him as an elite player, then last Sunday could be remembered as the day the Vikings became Peterson's team. The running back took an in-your-face approach to both coaches and teammates that showed a level of leadership he hadn't previously displayed.

His actions, though, still spoke louder than his words. Peterson had gained 64 yards on the 69-yard final drive. Eighteen of those yards had come after he had been hit. For the game, he gained 192 yards on 30 carries and caught passes for 33 more yards. His 225 "all-purpose" yards (combining running, catching passes, and returning kickoffs and punts) were nearly

70 percent of the entire Viking offense. ESPN.com reporter Kevin Seifert wrote after the game that "Peterson has developed into the rarest of stars: One who can single-handedly change the outcome of a game." Peterson told Seifert that the game was his most satisfying performance as an NFL player: "We pulled it out." Peterson later told *Sporting News* writer Steve Greenberg that he considered that game his greatest game.

FAMINE, FAMINE, FEAST

Seifert reported that Peterson said, "The whole game, the guys were telling me, 'Be patient.'" In the first three quarters, many of his carries were four yards or less. His coaches had urged him during the week of practice before the game not to force the action—get two or three yards and eventually the defense will crack. He could then run for a big gain or a touchdown— "to the house." Peterson calls it being satisfied with "famine, famine, feast." At the end, he had feasted on the Packer defense.

The game showed that Peterson was developing patience. On his game-winning touchdown run, Peterson waited for his blockers to work. He then cut up the field and not back into the surrounding defenders. He made a "one-cut," a run that uses only one change of direction. And his extraordinary conditioning helped him—he was as fast and strong at the end of the game as he was at the beginning.

After the game, head coach Childress told Seifert and other reporters that Peterson had inspired his offensive line: "Adrian had great trust in what he was doing and what he was seeing. The guys up front kind of get charged up when they know that they have that guy running behind them."

The team had rallied behind its new leader. It was not the first time that the extraordinary young man from a small town in east Texas had inspired his teammates and lifted his fans. And it would not be the last.

Running All Day in Palestine, Texas

Adrian Peterson's roots go deep into the land of Palestine, Texas. The small town 110 miles (177 kilometers) southeast of Dallas is surrounded by pine woods and sagebrush prairie. Its dogwood trees and historic homes are attractive, but it also mixes old and new businesses, from a railroad hub to a Wal-Mart distribution center. Very quickly, Palestine blends into a country setting. Adrian Peterson told writer Joe Wuebben, "I'm talking about the regular street turns to gravel, and that street turns to dirt."

Peterson is the child of two people from Palestine with big dreams that never came true. His mother, Bonita Brown, established herself as a track star as a young girl. She became a Texas high school sprint champion, winning four gold medals. She even competed for the U.S. Junior Olympic team in Korea.

Some family members think she might have been fast enough to make the U.S. Olympic team. But soon after she received a track scholarship to the University of Houston, she became pregnant. She gave birth to a son, Brian, in 1984, and then on March 21, 1985, she became the mother to another son, Adrian. All hopes of making the Olympics were soon gone.

The father of her two sons is also a remarkable athlete, named Nelson Peterson. The son of shrimp-boat workers, he was born in Palestine but grew up in Freeport, Texas, and Key West, Florida, as his parents followed their work. In Texas from June to November, he played football. While he was in Florida the rest of the year, he played basketball. He told *Tulsa World* reporter John Hoover, "I developed my toughness in Texas and my attitude in Florida." He was a good enough basketball player to become one of the all-time single-season scoring leaders at Idaho State University, and he had dreams of playing in the National Basketball Association (NBA). But after an accidental gunshot wound to his leg became infected, those dreams died. He returned to Palestine to work.

A BROTHER'S DEATH

Bonita and Nelson never married, and soon Bonita moved from Palestine to a Dallas apartment complex with her two young boys, Brian and Adrian. They lived with her sister and nephews. The two brothers were inseparable. They did everything together. They were also competitive. Family friend Steve Eudey told reporters that Adrian sometimes unplugged the Nintendo rather than lose to his brother. And they raced home from the school bus stop to their apartment, some 150 yards (137 meters). Adrian was fast, but his older brother was faster.

Close to his eighth birthday, however, Adrian's life was changed forever. Brian was riding on his bike near the apartment when he was hit by a drunken driver. Adrian was playing in the schoolyard nearby and saw what happened. He later

A gifted athlete himself, it was Nelson Peterson who steered his son toward football to lift his spirits. He also taught Adrian the value of conditioning and pushing himself physically. In 2009, Nelson posed with Adrian before the Pro Bowl game.

told *New York Times* reporter Thayer Evans that he ran to his brother's body, fell to his knees, and cradled Brian's head. He screamed for help and cried as he realized he couldn't wake his brother. Brian later died of his injuries. Adrian was in shock. Bonita told reporter John Hoover, "When Brian passed, there was a big part of him [Adrian] that was gone."

Bonita decided to move back with her son to Palestine to be closer to Adrian's grandmother and father. One day at his grandmother's house, the phone rang. It was Nelson, calling Adrian to tell him that he was signed up to play youth football and that he needed to go to the athletic center in Palestine to get his helmet and pads and find out which team he was playing for. Peterson told Hoover, "I remember it like yesterday." His father had not even asked if his son wanted to play football. He just knew it would be good for Adrian and might help him deal with the loss of his brother. Adrian's mother was worried that her son was not big enough to play with the older boys. She need not have worried. When she finally saw him in practice, she realized he could play with anyone.

GROWING UP FAST AND A COWBOY FAN

Nelson became an assistant coach on his son's youth football teams so he could be closer to him. He wanted his son to love football. Adrian's favorite team became the Dallas Cowboys. He liked to wear the jerseys of both Deion Sanders and Michael Irvin, each a strong personality as well as a Cowboy star. Neither was a running back, but both studied the game and became football analysts after their careers were over.

Nelson knew how important it was to balance athletics and academics, and he stressed that Adrian's grades had to be kept up if he expected to play football. When Adrian received his first F, on his fifth-grade report card, his father took action. The next Saturday at a game, Adrian put on his helmet, buckled his chin strap, and waited eagerly to get on the field. His number was never called. He told Hoover, "I'm on the sideline and didn't get to play. Didn't get to touch the field. . . . My dad kept me out the whole game." Peterson calls that day his worst football memory.

Some better memories, though, came from working out with his father. Getting and staying physically fit became a way for them to be together. They lifted weights at the local YMCA. Since Adrian couldn't afford real weights at home, he put sand or water in water jugs and fitted the jugs to the ends of a pipe. He did squats and lunges with the homemade weights. He gained leg strength by attaching a tire to a rope and pulling it up hills, running forward and backward. By the time he was 11, he was bigger and stronger than most youngsters his age. He also had a running partner: His aunt had a Great Dane that liked to chase him. Fear provided great motivation to be both fast and quick.

Adrian also got stronger by working on farms in and around Palestine. He baled hay and wrestled cows and steers, working his upper and lower body. His natural restlessness kept him in motion, and constant motion builds strength and endurance. He was becoming tough as well as fast.

When he was 12, his Anderson County Youth Football League team, the Cowboys, played in a championship tournament in Texarkana, Texas. His coach, Steve Eudey, told Hoover that he knew by then that Adrian was the best player in Palestine, but that weekend in a driving rain, he discovered that Adrian was also the best player in the region: "They ran him out of bounds, or he slipped a few times, or he would stop and they would gang up on him. But I don't remember Adrian ever being tackled." The Cowboys won the championship trophy, and Adrian was the most valuable player of the tournament. Eudey told some of his players on the way home that they would remember this game for the rest of their lives, partly because of the victory and partly because they could some day say that they played on the same team as Adrian Peterson.

The Texarkana tournament marked a turning point in Adrian's young life. He knew he could play football against anyone, and he began to realize that his dream of playing in the NFL was possible. Unlike his parents, he could make his dreams come true.

OVERCOMING ANOTHER SHOCK

Nelson Peterson continued to be a big part of his son's life, even though Bonita married a minister named Frankie Jackson in 1996 and Adrian lived with his mother and stepfather. Adrian wanted to remain loyal to his father and couldn't confide in or be close to his stepfather quite yet. While still dealing with his brother's death, though, he had a second tragic loss.

Nelson worked at the Wal-Mart distribution center but had another job as well, an illegal one. He was part of a group selling drugs, mostly crack cocaine. He was arrested once in 1991 and again in 1998 when federal agents broke down the front door of his Palestine home and hauled him off to jail. He was convicted of drug-related activities, and in March 1999, he was sentenced to 10 years in a federal prison in the same city, Texarkana, that Adrian remembered from his football tournament.

In an interview with Thayer Evans, Nelson said, "What I did was wrong. I take full responsibility for that." He said the lowest point of his life was having to tell his 12-year-old son that he was involved in selling drugs. He had to speak through a glass partition at a jail, and he told Adrian he loved him. His son responded, "Daddy, you know I love you." The two then had to go their separate ways, as they would so many more times over the next few years. Each departure tore at both father and son.

Nelson told *Minneapolis Star Tribune* reporter Mark Craig, "I was a young guy who made a mistake. . . . I never used them [drugs] myself." He went on to say that he knew he still had responsibilities for Adrian and his other children even though he was in prison. Nelson also said that prison might have saved his life. The drug world is a dangerous one, and in a strange way prison protected him from it.

Adrian struggled with this second loss, which seemed almost as permanent as the first. Yet again he had to endure what happened to him through no fault of his own. So he had to find a way to not let his sadness and anger get the best of him. He did not cut himself off from his father. Adrian vowed to visit Nelson frequently, and they spoke by phone at least twice a week. This contact made the son feel less confused and the father feel as though he had something to live for.

Adrian would later tell Associated Press reporters that he was "crushed by not having his father around, but never made that an excuse why he couldn't succeed." He now wanted to do better, to take more control of his life. His motto became, "No excuses." He began to set goals and meet them, one by one.

BECOMING A TRACK STAR

Bonita Jackson knew she had to help get her son through this tough time in his life. Just as his father helped him with his brother's death by giving him football, his mother helped with his father's incarceration by giving him track as a way of coping. She took Adrian to the school field and taught him how to run with discipline and force. She told *Minneapolis Star Tribune* writer Jim Souhan that she started with the basics, telling her son: "Stay focused. Look at the finish line. Don't look back, because if you take just an instant, you could look back and be in last place." She taught him to lean in and hug the edge of the track when running the 200-meter race. She was determined to make up for his father's absence and help guide him away from trouble.

By the time he became an eighth grader at Westwood Junior High in Palestine, Peterson was developing into a track star. At an early meet in Elkhart, he wasn't sure where he was supposed to take off from in the long jump, but he won the event anyway, almost jumping beyond the landing pit. He won several events in meets: The 100-meter sprint, the 200 meters, the triple jump, the long jump, and the 4x100 relay all became contests in which he could finish first.

Sometime between eighth grade and high school, he began to beat his mother in a sprint (they disagree on when exactly he finally won a race against her). When he got to high school, his track coach was amazed to find Peterson lowering his 100-meter time from 11.2 to 10.5 seconds in less than a year. His official time at a Texas state meet as a junior in high school was 10.33 seconds, the third-fastest time in the state that year. Family friend and mentor Steve Eudey thinks Peterson could have been an Olympic sprinter in the 200-meter dash and a world-class long jumper. But many family members say the 100-meter dash was his best event.

At a track meet in Miami, however, when he was a junior, Adrian had a life crisis as he flashed back to his brother's death and his father's life in prison. Bonita described it to *Chicago Tribune* reporter Melissa Isaacson:

> He called me three times in a row. You know your children, and I knew something was wrong. I said, "Baby, is everything all right?" He finally broke down and told me he was reliving everything. I'm trying to maintain control and I'm crying. Finally I got myself together and said, "It's OK, it's good to let it go."

The teenager had become overcome with grief. With the help of his mother, though, he got beyond his pain and turned it into fuel.

GUIDING A TRACK STAR TOWARD FOOTBALL

Jeff Harrell, the track coach, became the Palestine High School Wildcat football coach when Adrian was a junior. He knew how fast and strong Adrian was, so he designed

Peterson's mother was a track star whose potential was cut short. She taught her son the finer points of running, and Adrian soon set records in sprinting and the long jump. Above, Bonita Jackson sits beside Adrian after he signed a national letter of intent to play football for Oklahoma. Adrian's half-brother, Jaylon Jackson, stands between them.

an offense around him—the one-back system. After studying how the University of Oklahoma used its running backs, Harrell saw how to coordinate the linemen and the single running back so they worked as one unit. He placed Adrian several yards behind the quarterback and gave him enough room to see where the holes in the line were as the play developed. Giving the running back a better view of the defensive wall was important, and having a back with the ability to quickly scan the field ahead of him was key. Strength and power were not enough. "Field vision," reading the defense, counted as well.

It was a simple and basic offensive football strategy, and it worked. Adrian made it work. The rest became school football history.

Being successful, however, required more work and discipline than most people could imagine. First, Adrian's natural gifts had to be brought under control, like a Jedi knight learning discipline to use the forces within him. For example, Adrian was so fast that he got the quarterback's handoff too quickly on some plays. So, he had to be moved farther from the line of scrimmage, and the blocks would need to be timed so he could take advantage of them. Most football fans know that a quarterback and his receivers have to be in sync. Fewer fans know that the running back and his linemen also need to carefully coordinate their moves. They are partners in a run-dance.

Adrian's running style soon reminded fans in Texas of the NFL great Eric Dickerson, who was also fast and strong. So, Adrian asked the Palestine equipment manager for No. 29 in honor of Dickerson. The school did not have that number, so he settled for No. 28 instead. He wears that number even today.

HIGH SCHOOL FOOTBALL IN TEXAS

Texas high school football is legendary for its excitement and its huge crowds for Friday night games played under the lights. Adrian increased the excitement level in every game he played. All of his hard work in pushing his body to its limits in training, all of the coaching he had received, and all of his natural ability came together to create an almost perfect football running machine.

In his first varsity football game when he was a junior, Adrian ran for 212 yards. In his second game, he ran for an astonishing 340 yards. He was just a blur in the backfield, he was getting to the line so quickly. By the fourth game of the season, word had spread and offers for college scholarships were already starting to come in. In four short weeks, Adrian had exploded to statewide fame, and the ripples kept spreading. Coach Harrell found his office door half-covered with Post-It notes from college recruiters asking questions about Adrian. But he also had phone calls from Nelson, who urged Harrell to make sure Adrian kept his grades up. And Nelson could be counted on to give his son a wake-up call any time Nelson felt he needed one.

By the end of his junior year, Adrian had gained 2,051 yards and scored 22 touchdowns. He averaged 8.3 yards a carry, an incredible accomplishment—5 yards a carry at any level of

ERIC DICKERSON: THE MODEL FOR ADRIAN PETERSON

Before there was Adrian Peterson, there was Eric Dickerson, also one of the most exciting running backs college and professional football have ever seen. The two backs have many similarities.

Dickerson was born in a small Texas town named Sealy and had an unsettled early life: His mother was only 17 when she gave birth to him, and she couldn't cope at first. So, Eric's great aunt Viola adopted him. He thought for years that his mother was Viola and that his real mother was his older sister.

Dickerson was skinny and had poor vision when he was a child, so the other kids teased him. He didn't fit in. But he began to lift weights and work out as a way of getting control in his life. By the time he entered eighth grade, he had also found football. He later told reporters that he was terrified at first when he ran the ball—he felt he was running for his life. But he became a Texas high school football star, as well as a track standout.

Dickerson wanted to go to the University of Oklahoma, just as Peterson later would. But Dickerson's aunt wanted him closer to home, so he went to Southern Methodist University (SMU). He excelled there and was drafted by the Los Angeles Rams as football is considered exceptional. He was even better in his senior year: He gained 2,960 yards and scored 32 touchdowns. Adrian's average of 11.7 yards a carry that year was the stuff of legends.

He had the ability to change directions and not lose speed. He was never afraid to run right up the middle and take on big

the No. 2 pick in the 1983 NFL Draft (after quarterback John Elway). Initially, he was so nervous that he fumbled six times in his first three NFL games. He settled down, though, and used his speed and power well: He ran for 1,808 yards as a rookie, a record Peterson would later shoot for.

In his second year, 1984, he set the all-time single-season rushing record of 2,105 yards. He gave each of his offensive linemen a gold ring encrusted with diamonds and the number "2,105." He led the NFL in rushing four times in his 11-year career and reached the 10,000-yard mark faster than any running back in history.

Dickerson was a sight to behold when he ran. Like Peterson, he was tall (almost 6-foot-3, or 1.91 meters) so he wore a neck pad as a brace for protection. His vision needed correction, so he wore prescription goggles and a sun visor that made him look like an astronaut. He ran upright, much as Peterson does, so he could see better.

One coach described him as being like a lion on the prowl, hunting for the end zone. Fans called him "Eric the Great." He was a hero of Peterson's and of many children who wanted to overcome life's early difficulties and achieve greatness.

linemen. Like Eric Dickerson, he seemed to be like a lion on the prowl, hunting for the end zone. Adrian also had what coaches call "runner's vision"—the ability to see not just where cracks in the defense are, but where they are going to be. It is part instinct and part a special sight.

In his final game as a high school player, he gained 350 yards—in the first half. The game was such a blowout that Harrell sat him for the second half. The coach, though, saw that his star wasn't acting like a star. The coach later told reporter Isaacson, "Adrian knows he's blessed, but he just takes it in stride."

Football and track, however, were not Peterson's whole life in high school. He was social and popular by all accounts. He and some of his friends and teammates would eat at the Cotton Patch Cafe on Fridays before a game. He usually ordered chicken-fried steak and mashed potatoes. And he had many girlfriends, including Domanique King. She told reporter Thayer Evans that she had competition for his attention. "There were just too many girls," she said. He was a good-looking athlete whose life experiences had made him humble and sympathetic to others.

BEING NAMED A HIGH SCHOOL ALL-AMERICAN

Peterson became a high school All-American, a very prestigious honor. One of the people who decide which players get to be All-American high school football players is Tom Lemming. He helps pick the high school all-stars for ESPN and the All-USA High School Football Team for *USA Today*.

In 1978, at the age of 23, Lemming decided that he wanted to be a high school football scout. Unlike Major League Baseball, football had few scouts looking at high school players. He reasoned that he would visit as many players as he could, compile a list of the best, and sell the list to college football coaches. In the days before videotapes, the Internet, and cell phones, most coaches were only hearing about local players.

Coach Bear Bryant of the University of Alabama recruited players in the South. Coach Bo Schembechler at the University of Michigan looked at players from the Midwest. Lemming thought he could change that.

Slowly coaches began to realize the value of what he did. He provided them with a competitive advantage. He was a good evaluator of talent. As the ways to get and process information improved, Lemming's job became easier. By the time Peterson was in high school, Lemming had the making of his All-American team down to a science: He narrows down the field of some 3 million high school players using a vast network of coaches he knows. Then he collects data on the Internet and watches thousands of hours of video. He personally interviews about 1,500 candidates, selecting 100 of those as top prospects. He finally chooses roughly 25 as "All-Americans."

Lemming and several others knew that Peterson was one of the best high school running backs in the country in 2003. Being one of the best in high school carries over to college and professional football. Writer Michael Lewis noted in *The Blind Side* that in some years more than half of Lemming's high school All-Americans later become first-round draft picks in the NFL.

FINDING THE RIGHT COLLEGE

The stakes were high for many colleges as they recruited Peterson. College coaches need to figure out what is most important for both a player and his family. The University of Oklahoma's coach, Bob Stoops, figured out that Nelson was a key to recruiting his son. So, he and several of his assistant coaches visited Nelson and Adrian in an outside visitors area at the Texarkana federal prison on the first day that coaches were allowed to visit recruits (the first day of the recruit's senior year). It was a crucial meeting in helping Adrian decide, he told reporter Thayer Evans: "That showed a lot of commitment by Coach Stoops coming and talking to my dad." The Oklahoma

Peterson was named a high school All-American in 2003, an honor that often carries over to success in the NFL Draft. When he decided to play for Oklahoma, many considered him the top recruit in the country.

coaches told Peterson that they wanted him and needed him, but they were going to win with or without him. He and his father liked their honesty.

The University of Oklahoma football teams have had more wins than any other college team since World War II. And they have seven national championships. Both Petersons knew it was an elite program that would train and coach a running back well.

When coaches from the University of Southern California, the University of Texas, Louisiana State University, and many other universities tried to set up interviews with Nelson, prison officials decided the disruption was too much for guards to handle and so all other coaches were denied access. The schools and coaches were not happy.

Reporter John Hoover wrote that Nelson and Adrian at some point sat down and wrote their college choice on a piece of paper. Nelson wrote, "Whatever decision you make, I'll be happy." Adrian wrote, "The University of Oklahoma." But he didn't make his decision public right away.

PLAYING IN HIS FIRST BOWL GAME

On January 3, 2004, Peterson went to San Antonio, Texas, to play in the prestigious U.S. Army All-American Bowl. The best high school seniors from the East and West compete every year in the Alamodome. ESPN's Gene Wojciechowski reported that one of the players on the East team, Peterson's opponent, taunted Peterson and said he was overrated. He tried to provoke the running back into a fight, but it didn't work. Peterson had control of his emotions. Like a good Jedi warrior, he knew how to pick his battles.

One of Peterson's runs that day made *SportsCenter's* top-10 plays: Peterson received the ball from the quarterback, and 10 defenders swarmed around him in his own backfield. He was trapped. Somehow, he broke free to the sideline, faked an inside move to freeze the safety, and outran everyone to the end zone.

Against the nation's best, he gained 95 yards and scored two touchdowns. Near the end of the game, he put on a baseball cap that had the University of Oklahoma logo. The world finally knew which college he was going to. The Oklahoma coaching staff could finally rejoice.

Peterson was soon named the top high school player in the country by several news organizations. He was also awarded the Hall Trophy as the U.S. Army National Player of the Year. His potential seemed almost unlimited. But the change from high school to college football is a major challenge for many players. Peterson was ready to find out if he could meet that challenge. His search for greatness entered new territory.

The Oklahoma Years

When Adrian Peterson arrived at an apartment near the University of Oklahoma in Norman in 2004, he didn't have much with him—his clothes and a picture of his brother, Brian, and not much else. As he unpacked the family car, he told his mother not to cry. He said he was going to be all right and she shouldn't worry.

The next day he showed up at the university's indoor workout facility and met the legendary and tough trainer Jerry Schmidt, who looks like a Marine drill instructor. ESPN writer Gene Wojciechowski reported that Schmidt recalled the meeting clearly and that Peterson's basic physical tests were unusual:

> "He's [Peterson] got on some funky high-tops and old shorts. The guy never asks what we were going

to do, and then he does a 39-inch vertical [jump], a 10'7" broad jump." Schmidt pauses to let the numbers sink in. "He runs [a 40-yard dash in] 4.43, 4.42. He's a freak."

The Oklahoma offensive coordinator, Chuck Long, told reporter Melissa Isaacson that freshmen usually have a difficult time with the Sooners' football conditioning program. Many go back home and wait to grow a little stronger. But Peterson was different. He was often finishing with the leaders in whatever exercise they were doing: "For a true freshman to be able to do that is very rare."

At the age of 19, Peterson was nearing his physical peak. He was almost 6-foot-2 (1.88 m) and roughly 215 pounds (98 kilograms), mostly pure muscle with very little body fat. He had been training hard ever since he was young. And now he had access to state-of-the-art training equipment and techniques. He traded up from homemade weights to the latest in muscle-building weight-training machines. He was only going to get stronger.

Peterson worked hard on each leg muscle group in the weight room, doing lunges and squats with more than 300 pounds (136 kg). He began to stay after football workouts or practice and run across the field from one sideline to the other and back again, over and over. He concentrated on having an explosive start, his now-famous boost phase. Peterson still doesn't like treadmills or stationary bikes: He would rather run outside and work up a good sweat.

THE 2004 SEASON BEGINS

The 2004 Oklahoma Sooners promised to be an excellent team, ranking second in the nation in the preseason polls. Their quarterback, Jason White, won the Heisman Trophy the year before, an award given to the best player in college football. Their starting running back, Kejuan Jones, was very good, and their offensive line was intact from the year before. Few freshmen would be able to crack this lineup.

Oklahoma opened the 2004 season playing Bowling Green University at home in Norman, in the Gaylord Family-Oklahoma Memorial Stadium. The stadium holds more than 80,000 spectators, making it one of the largest in the country (it held 500 when it opened in 1923). It can be an intimidating place to play.

Oklahoma was as good as advertised in the polls. White completed most of his passes, and Jones ran for 147 yards on 32 carries. Peterson also played, scoring a 35-yard touchdown on a brilliant run. He gained 100 yards on 16 carries, a solid effort for his first college game. Yet he also made mistakes: He fumbled twice on his first six carries, but he recovered both fumbles. Oklahoma won easily, 40-24.

That game began an extraordinary streak for the freshman. He improved in his second game, rushing for 117 yards and two touchdowns against the University of Houston. Oklahoma won even more easily than the week before, 63-13. The next week, on September 18 against Oregon, Peterson ran for a remarkable 183 yards.

The following week Peterson started for the first time, against Texas Tech. He gained 146 yards, and the Sooners won a hard-fought game, 28-13. Peterson was the first Oklahoma player ever to run for 100 or more yards in his first four games. Next up, though, was the biggest game of the season.

THE RED RIVER RIVALRY

One of the great football rivalries is called the Red River Rivalry or the Red River Showdown (also known for years as the Red River Shootout), between the University of Texas Longhorns and Oklahoma. Ten times since 1950, the winner of the game has gone on to be the national champion. Like the Florida-Georgia game, it is played at a neutral site because of the intense fan interest.

Peterson had an unusual group of fans who would watch this game with even more intensity than normal. The inmates at the Texarkana federal prison always reserved a special seat in front of the television for Nelson Peterson. Even some of the Texas fans in prison would be rooting for his son.

The 2004 showdown between Oklahoma and Texas was played on October 9 at the Cotton Bowl in Dallas, Texas. The stadium was divided at the 50-yard line into two enormous groups: Half the people wore crimson and cream, the Sooner colors, while the other half dressed in the Longhorn orange and white.

BOOMERS VERSUS SOONERS

Owning land has always been a piece of the American Dream. That dream led some 20,000 people in wagons, on horses, and on foot to the Texas and Kansas borders of the Oklahoma Territory in 1889. They were there to claim plots of free land (about 6,000 parcels were up for grabs) measuring some 160 acres each.

The people came from all parts of America and the world—doctors, lawyers, gamblers, crooks, city people looking for wide open spaces and a new start, country people who found Texas and Kansas too tame, young married couples, single men and women, and anyone else not afraid of adventure. The book *Cimarron* by Edna Ferber and the movie *Far and Away* (starring Tom Cruise and Nicole Kidman) describe the incredible scene, one of American history's most famous.

At high noon on April 22, the Oklahoma Land Rush began. U.S. Army Cavalry soldiers dressed in blue uniforms shot pistols or cannons at various starting points, and the stampede was on. The "boomers" rushed out into the land looking for the

The coaches had put in a new play for Peterson, the "Fling," that got Peterson quickly to the outside of the field, where he could use his speed. On his first play, he used the Fling to gain 44 yards down the right sideline. The Longhorns never completely recovered. Peterson ended up with an incredible 225 yards on 32 carries. He dominated the game, grinding and fighting for extra yards. His running let Oklahoma keep the ball away from the Texas offense. The final score was 12-0, in favor of Oklahoma.

The Texas coach, Mack Brown, looked for Peterson after the game to shake his hand. He knew his team had played

best spots—grasslands near rivers and the railroad, on higher ground. What they often found were the "sooners," people who had come into the territory without permission before April 22. These were often land surveyors and railroad workers. Sometimes, gunfights settled the disputes that followed. It was years before the mess of conflicting land claims between boomers and sooners was settled.

At first, "sooner" had a strongly negative meaning—someone who cheated. Within a few years, however, that connotation changed. A "sooner" came to mean someone who had ambition as well as a can-do attitude. The fact that sooners owned a sizable portion of Oklahoma may have had something to do with the shift. When the newly formed University of Oklahoma adopted "Sooner" as its name in 1908 (the year after Oklahoma became a state), the word no longer carried any negative meanings. On the other hand, "boomer" has picked up some negative overtones over the years.

Peterson (28) slips from the tackle by Texas defensive end Brian Robison (39) during a 2004 game. The Sooner running back ran 225 yards on 32 carries for the game.

against an extraordinary athlete. As always, Peterson talked with his father after the game. Nelson always saw ways to help his son improve. Adrian Peterson told Melissa Isaacson, "After every game he calls me and tells me things he saw [on television]. Even if I break off a big run, he tells me little things I did wrong, like not switching the ball over [carrying the ball in the hand facing away from the defender]. He sees things like that and I appreciate it." Peterson, though, had not done much wrong in the Texas game. And he knew performances like this one were giving his father hope, a reason to look forward to the day he would be free. Nelson knew that better days were coming because of his son's ability to run all day.

A HEISMAN TROPHY CANDIDATE

The next two weeks, in games against Kansas State and Kansas, Peterson kept his streak alive: He had now rushed for more than 100 yards in all seven of his games. He was averaging 146.1 yards a game.

His next great performance came in Stillwater, Oklahoma, on October 30, 2004, when the Sooners played the Oklahoma State Cowboys. The in-state rivalry has heated up in recent years since Oklahoma State has become a consistent football powerhouse. The game was close. Oklahoma was ahead by only a touchdown in the third quarter when Peterson took a handoff near his own 20-yard line, spun out of a tackle, burst through the line of defenders, and sprinted away from everybody for an 80-yard touchdown. ESPN reporter Gene Wojciechowski called the spin-move an instant legend. On his next carry, Peterson gained 56 more yards. With that run, he broke the Oklahoma freshman rushing record of 1,184 yards set by De'Mond Parker in 1996.

The Oklahoma State defense had actually concentrated on stopping Peterson throughout the game. But it couldn't. He gained 196 yards in the second half alone (161 of them in the third quarter) and ended up with 249 yards, helping Oklahoma win its closest game of the year, 38-35. His team was undefeated, and he had gained 1,272 yards in eight games.

The next week, the 8–0 Sooners traveled to College Station, Texas, to play Texas A&M. Peterson suffered a dislocated shoulder in the game, one of the most painful injuries a running back can have. Late in the fourth quarter, his team had the ball with a third down and two yards to go for a first down. It was a crucial play. A trainer had popped Peterson's shoulder back into place, but it was throbbing and sore. He came back into the game, took the ball, and bulled his way for a four-yard gain. The pain must have been agonizing. But his team had the first down and went on to win, 42-35.

Peterson led his team to a 12–0 record and the Big 12 championship in his first year as a college player. In the game for the right to go to the national championship, Peterson had runs of 18 and 24 yards in the first drive against Colorado. Oklahoma demolished the Buffaloes, 42-3.

Peterson had been so spectacular that he became a Heisman Trophy candidate in his freshman year, a rare achievement. On the night of December 11, 2004, at New York's Hilton Hotel, Peterson sat on the stage overlooking an enormous third-floor ballroom. ESPN broadcast the ceremony. He was with several other Heisman finalists, including his teammate Jason White, University of Southern California (USC) running back Reggie Bush, USC quarterback Matt Leinart, and University of Utah quarterback Alex Smith. When the voting was announced, Leinart won, and Peterson came in second, the highest finish ever by a freshman. He would later say that New York was his favorite city to visit.

A FINAL DISAPPOINTMENT

Oklahoma played for the national championship against USC on January 4, 2005, in the Orange Bowl held at Pro Player Stadium in Miami, Florida. Both teams were undefeated, and for the first time, two Heisman Trophy winners (White and Leinart) would be facing each other in the national title game. The matchup between USC running back Reggie Bush and Peterson was also a story—two of the best running backs in college football would test great run defenses.

Oklahoma scored first, but then USC took over. Taking advantage of four turnovers, Leinart threw three touchdown passes in the second quarter alone. Bush ran well, and by half-time the USC Trojans led 38-10.

The game was so lopsided that fans were restless. They even booed singer Ashlee Simpson during her halftime song "La La." Oklahoma just could not stop the USC offense. Because they were so far behind, the Sooners had to gamble with longer passes and could not run as much. They fell even further behind. Peterson was held to 82 yards on 25 carries. The final score was 55-19, a crushing defeat for the Sooners. It was listed by reporter John Hoover as one of Peterson's worst college memories. Nelson told Wojciechowski, "He was ready to come home that night. Now he has to start over and work harder."

Despite the loss, Peterson had one of the best seasons a college freshman running back has ever had. He ran for 1,925 yards and 15 touchdowns. All of college football knew who he was, and even the pros were taking notice. Many NFL teams would be keeping an eye on this phenom.

Yet his body had also paid a price: Soon after the Orange Bowl, Peterson had to have surgery on his left shoulder to repair ligament damage to it. He had run all season with a tough determination that turned his upper body into a battering ram against oncoming tacklers. He used his shoulders to move tacklers out of the way. His body, though, had to obey the laws of physics—for every hit he delivered, he received an equal and opposite one. He had taken a good deal of punishment, and it was only the start of what was to come.

THE 2005 SEASON

Eleven Sooners were drafted by the NFL in April 2005, which made 2005 a rebuilding year for the team. As great as Peterson was, he needed good blockers and an experienced quarterback who could throw the football well enough to keep the defense

In 2004, the Heisman Trophy candidates attended the awards ceremony in New York City. From left: Alex Smith, Reggie Bush, Matt Leinart, Adrian Peterson, and Jason White. Leinart won the award. White had won the trophy the year before, and Bush won the following year.

from stacking up against him. He lost most of those teammates to pro football.

The first game of the 2005 season was a disaster. Peterson injured his right ankle during the contest against Texas Christian University (TCU), and he was limited to 63 yards, the second lowest total of his college career. Oklahoma lost that game, but Peterson fought back in the next game, against the University of Tulsa on September 10. Tulsa led 9-7 in the third quarter, but then Peterson took over. He carried the ball nine times in a 10-play scoring drive. He ran the ball 10 more times in the next drive, scoring on a spectacular 41-yard run. For the game, he ran for 220 yards and three touchdowns on 32 carries. He carried the team's offense, and Oklahoma won, 31-15.

Great athletes need to score, not just do well. They want to get the reward for their play. Derek Jeter touching home plate, Michael Jordan hitting a three-pointer, and Emmitt Smith slashing into the end zone are sports highlights. So, like many great running backs, scoring touchdowns became most important to Peterson, more important to him than long runs. He lowered his shoulders, driving to break tackles, in search of the end zone. He was relentless and at times unstoppable.

Against Kansas State on October 1, though, his body once again paid a high price for his efforts. Early in the second quarter, Peterson ran hard into the middle of the line for a two-yard gain. Both a defender and a teammate collapsed on his right ankle, severely spraining it. A sprained ankle can sometimes be a more severe injury than a broken one, since bones can often heal faster than ligaments. He missed most of the next four games, including a 45-12 loss in the Red River Rivalry.

Peterson pushed his body as much as he dared during his recovery. Players and trainers try to know when an injury has healed enough to allow playing time. They usually can't wait for complete recovery—the pressure to play is just too great.

Peterson's ankle was not fully healed by the time Oklahoma played in-state rival Oklahoma State on November 26. So he amazed even his fans: He ran for an 84-yard touchdown in the third quarter, followed by a 71-yard score. For the game, he ran for an impressive 237 yards. Oklahoma won, 42-14. He was back with a vengeance.

Oklahoma ended its season at 8–4, and Peterson had done well by most standards, despite his injury. He had gained 1,108 yards and scored 14 touchdowns, only one fewer than his sensational first year. But he averaged fewer yards per carry in 2005 (5.0) than in 2004 (5.7). He knew he could do better.

LIFE GETS MORE COMPLICATED

During the spring of 2006, Peterson found himself at the center of a small controversy. College players on scholarship (the school pays for tuition and room and board) are not allowed to receive unearned money or large gifts from supporters of the team or anyone else other than family. Peterson had driven a Lexus from a local dealer without paying for it, and school officials had to worry about whether he had violated NCAA rules. He had not, though, since he worked at the dealership part-time in the summer and had not received any extra money. Two other teammates, however, were in violation and were kicked off the team.

Soon after, Peterson bought a 1983 Oldsmobile for less than $2,000, painted it red, and named it "Old School." He told Thayer Evans: "There's a difference between things you want and things you need." He needed a car. But he also wanted things. By now it was clear that he wanted a professional career.

He also had a new responsibility, a baby named Ade'ja. Peterson has never talked to reporters about the baby's mother, but he wanted to be a good parent and help care for both mother and child. Suddenly the world of his adolescence was being left behind. He was a young adult, growing up quickly. His life was getting more complicated.

As always, he worked hard to stay in shape for the upcoming season. He never would let himself get soft. His body was the one thing he could control. So when the first game of the 2006 season came, he was ready.

THE 2006 SEASON GETS UNDERWAY

Against the University of Alabama at Birmingham (UAB), Peterson ran for 139 yards and one touchdown and caught a pass for 69 more yards and another touchdown. The Sooners won, 24-17, and beat the University of Washington the next week. Peterson was named "Big 12 Offensive Player of the Week" for his 165-yard performance. He was off to a great start.

Oklahoma, though, lost a strange game in Eugene, Oregon, when officials made an error about who recovered an onside kick. Oregon was given the ball and scored a touchdown to win, 34-33. The officials were later suspended after replays showed that they had made the wrong decision about the onside kick. The loss hurt.

The 2006 season delivered another blow: Texas quarterback Colt McCoy proved why he was a Heisman Trophy candidate, saving one of his best games for the Red River Showdown. Peterson had a dazzling 29-yard touchdown in the second quarter: He ran straight up the middle, made one cut, and was gone. His 109 yards for the game, though, were not enough to overcome McCoy's passing. The Sooners lost the big game, 28-10.

Nelson Peterson told his son after the game, as reported by Associated Press sports writer Jeff Latzke, "You've got a long season ahead. Push forward, be a leader." And both father and son knew the next game was special.

THE REUNION GAME: OCTOBER 14, 2006

Nelson Peterson was released from prison, and a dream now came true: He could go to a game and watch his son play in person for the first time since Adrian was 12. That dream had helped him get through his eight years behind bars. It came true on October 14, 2006.

The reunion game was in Norman against the Iowa State Cyclones. Author Stephen Currie, in *Adrian Peterson*, noted that Peterson spoke to reporters before the game about his father: "Even though he was away so long, he was with me in spirit. . . . He's my father, and he never stopped being that. Even though he made mistakes, I love him and I am proud of how he's turning his life around."

Peterson told Latzke that he expected to get an extra boost knowing that his father was going to be in the stands: "I'm going to be pumped up. . . . It's a real big deal." And a pumped-up Adrian Peterson is nearly unstoppable. The first time he touched the ball, he ran for 40 yards. Two plays later he scored a touchdown. He ran around and through the Iowa State defense.

But the joy of having his father watch him in person was replaced by a crushing disappointment in one play. After a spectacular 53-yard run during which Peterson cut between and ran over defenders, he approached the goal line and launched himself into the end zone in a superhuman effort to avoid one last tackler. He needed and wanted to score. But his leg was hit in midair, twisting him. He landed awkwardly, and his shoulder took the full force of the landing. His collarbone snapped into two pieces. The Oklahoma fans, and his father, were stunned into silence.

As rapidly as his spirits had soared at having his father at the game, they plunged knowing he was going to miss the rest of the season. To make matters worse, his mother fell and broke her leg in two places later that day at a family reunion. Bonita told John Hoover, "I'm OK. I'm just worried about him. I just want to be there for him."

A BIG DECISION

Doctors said that Peterson would be unable to play for about eight weeks. People began to speculate whether Peterson would forgo his senior year and enter the NFL Draft. Many football experts expected that he would immediately sign with an agent to move ahead with the business of becoming a professional football player. He was sure to be a top draft pick for 2007, and each of those players would be expected to get more than $40 million. If he signed with an agent, however, he would not be able to play in a bowl game and he wouldn't be able to play for Oklahoma in his senior year.

Peterson and his father and other family members carefully weighed the options. He loved playing at Oklahoma and was popular with both fans and teammates. According to author Stephen Currie, Oklahoma coach Bob Stoops said at the time that Peterson is "a guy that's popular in the locker room because of how he works and his attitude."

But he now had the most serious injury of his young life, and another one could put his pro football career at risk. His dreams could be smashed, like his parents' dreams had been. In addition, Peterson had a child and a family to help financially. He had to consider them. So, he finally decided that he would sign with an agent and enter the NFL Draft but only after he played one last college game, the 2007 Fiesta Bowl in Glendale, Arizona.

THE 2007 FIESTA BOWL

When Peterson took the field at the University of Phoenix Stadium on January 1, 2007, in the Fiesta Bowl, he was taking a big risk of injuring himself more seriously, but he felt that he owed it to his teammates. The Sooners, with a record of 11–2, were playing another good team, undefeated Boise State University. The game is now considered a classic.

The Boise State Broncos led at halftime, 21-10. Then they scored again, putting the Sooners behind by 18 points. Oklahoma came roaring back with Peterson's running and some good passing to take the lead by a touchdown with a minute to go. Then, Boise State scored on a trick play—called the hook and ladder (one player catches a pass and then pitches the ball to another running by him)—with 18 seconds to go. The game was tied, 35-35, so it went into overtime.

On the first play in the extra period, Peterson scored a touchdown. As usual, he seemed to be as strong at the end of the game as at the beginning. The Sooners led, 42-35. Unlike the sudden death of overtime in pro football, college games allow both teams a chance to score in overtime. The Broncos answered with a touchdown of their own. But they chose to go for a two-point conversion after the touchdown, to win or lose the game on one play. In a play still shown on ESPN highlights,

Peterson (28) scores a touchdown on the first play of overtime against Boise State during the 2007 Fiesta Bowl, his last college game. He ended his three-year college career with 4,045 yards gained and 41 touchdowns scored.

the Boise State quarterback dropped back, faked a pass, and handed the ball behind his back to a running back streaking by. The "Statue of Liberty" play worked. The runner scored, and Boise State won a thriller, 43-42.

With that play, Peterson's college career was over. He was among the leaders in the Oklahoma record books: 4,045 yards gained, third-best all-time for a Sooner running back, only 26 behind Joe Washington and 73 short of Billy Sims's totals; 41 touchdowns scored; 5.4 yards a carry on average; more than 130 yards a game. His numbers are especially impressive because Peterson spent only three years in college while the other record-holders spent four.

It was time, however, to set other records, in games that had even bigger and faster players than college. He was going pro. He announced on January 15, 2007, that he was going to enter the NFL Draft and not stay at Oklahoma for his senior year. Oklahoma's loss was the NFL's gain.

Becoming a Feared Viking

The best college football players in the country are invited by an NFL committee to the National Invitational Camp, better known as the "Combine." Some 300 players come to Indianapolis, Indiana, during the last week of February to see and be seen by NFL coaches, scouts, and executives. The players are tested physically, mentally, and psychologically. After the Combine, each team rates a player according to whether and when the team should pick him in an annual process in April known as the NFL Draft.

Every team knew that Adrian Peterson was one of the top players in the country. Teams, though, had two worries about him. First, he had been injured three times in college and his not-yet-healed collarbone was almost certainly reinjured during the Fiesta Bowl. His running style meant that defensive players would repeatedly hit him, and he was not so big by pro standards that he could take excessive punishment. Second, and even more important, he had rarely caught passes at Oklahoma—only 24 in three years. Pro football is filled with pass-oriented offenses. Running backs need to be able to catch the ball as well as run with it. They also need to pass-block for their quarterback and run precise routes that depend on timing. The college game forgave mistakes more than the pro game would.

While he sat in a hotel in downtown Indianapolis the night before the Combine began, Peterson was hit with another family tragedy. He learned that his stepbrother, Chris Paris, had been murdered in Houston. Peterson thought about returning home immediately, but he remembered a conversation he had with his stepbrother just a few days before. Paris has said for him to represent Palestine, Texas, and the family well. He decided he needed to stay and perform. There was no turning back now, not even for the death of a beloved family member.

One executive at the 2007 Combine, Cleveland Browns general manager Phil Savage, told *USA Today*, "Unfortunately, when tragedy strikes, the world doesn't stop. Adrian was able to go out and perform despite his loss." Peterson ran the all-important 40-yard dash in 4.38 and 4.40 seconds, showing his blazing speed. He caught passes as well, both from the backfield as a runner and from the wide receiver position flanked out to the side of the field. His injuries seemed as if they were in the past.

His stock rose at the Combine and later during "pro day" at the University of Oklahoma when NFL scouts tested him and some teammates. General managers and running backs coaches around the league now had more data to go with their study of his game films. They also saw that Peterson was mature, polite, and honest in his conversations with all of these new people.

Associated Press sportswriter Jeff Latzke interviewed Peterson after the Combine and before the NFL Draft. Peterson told him, "All the hard work, sweat, blood, and tears that came along the way, it's starting to pay off. That's why I work—to be the best." He also knew that his attitude was important. "You always have to improve. I never have sat back and just been satisfied in my game."

GETTING DRAFTED BY MINNESOTA

The 2007 NFL Player Selection Meeting, better known as "the Draft," took place on April 28 and 29 at New York City's Radio City Music Hall, showing just how popular a spectator event it had become. ESPN and the NFL Network both covered the spectacle. Fans were given free tickets after waiting countless hours in line.

Like several potential high draft picks, Peterson had flown to New York in advance. His agent, Ben Dogra, already had a Nike sponsorship deal for him. Peterson made several appearances for the company. He still has a very rewarding deal with Nike.

When the first day of the draft came, Peterson tried to relax with his family at Radio City. He had done all he could do. A young lifetime of work was about to be rewarded. He watched and waited for his name to be called. Most draft experts expected quarterback JaMarcus Russell to be picked first, and he was. Some people thought Peterson would be the third selection and go to the Cleveland Browns. But they chose another player. Finally, with the seventh pick, NFL commissioner Roger Goodell came to the podium and announced that the Minnesota Vikings had chosen Adrian Peterson. He was the first running back to be taken. He was thrilled.

Viking coach Brad Childress told reporters, "We're obviously elated to have this guy. He is an explosive football player that can take it to the house [score a touchdown] from any point on the football field." Childress called Peterson "electric."

The Vikings flew Peterson and his parents to their Winter Park facility in Eden Prairie, Minnesota. Peterson sat between his mother and father as he talked to *Star Tribune* writer Mark Craig and others: "I got a little bit of my mom in me. . . . She's got a heart of gold. My dad raised me to be a man. He wasn't there for me physically, but mentally he was there." Bonita Jackson said, "Adrian's a pretty unique kid. He's had big obstacles to overcome in his life." Peterson was finally right where he wanted to be, with his mother and father and his new team. He had made it to the promised land of his dreams.

STRIKING IT RICH

In June 2007, thousands of people in Palestine lined Main Street for a parade honoring Peterson. At Palestine High School Wildcat Stadium, he told the crowd, "I am going to represent Palestine to my fullest." The local Wal-Mart was well stocked with his purple No. 28 Vikings jersey and a T-shirt that had images of him in uniform and his autograph. He was becoming a full-fledged celebrity.

His agent's job was to make him a rich man as well as a famous one. Dogra negotiated with the Vikings for several months, while Peterson worked out in Norman to stay in shape. He was used to the wonderful facilities there, and since he was not yet officially a Viking, he could not use their workout center.

Finally, on July 29, Dogra, Peterson, and the Vikings made a deal: Peterson would make $40.5 million over five years if he was successful, with a guarantee of $17 million. Unlike athletes in virtually every other pro sport, NFL players often don't get paid if they are injured or don't perform to certain levels. So, the only money they can count on is the guaranteed money. Peterson was now a wealthy man; after years of having very little money, he now had a great deal.

He was able to give back to his parents. He wanted to help his mother get the home of her dreams, so he bought his mother and stepfather a very comfortable house in the Houston area. He soon gave his father a metallic gray BMW. He could now satisfy both wants and needs, for the first time in his

In 2007, the Minnesota Vikings selected Peterson in the NFL Draft. The Sooner was the seventh pick in the draft's first round. Above, an elated Peterson holds a Vikings jersey during the draft at Radio City Music Hall.

life. He would soon buy himself a black-on-black Bentley. "Old School" had to go.

HIS FIRST PRO TRAINING CAMP

The day after he signed his contract, Peterson reported to the Vikings' training camp at Minnesota State University in Mankato. The beautiful campus is about 75 miles (121 km) south of Minneapolis. He was coming to camp later than most because of the complicated contract negotiations, and he needed to make up for lost time.

One of the first people he met was the Vikings' running backs coach, Eric Bieniemy. The coach was waiting eagerly because expectations for Peterson ran high. The rookie would have to get to know offensive plays and techniques more complicated than anything he had seen before.

Many NFL players describe how difficult the transition to pro football can be. During the day they have to practice more than they ever have, often twice a day. Their bodies are pushed to their physical limits. At night, players have to study complicated playbooks that can run hundreds of pages. The rookies get hazed, yelled at, humiliated, and overwhelmed. They spend countless hours in meeting rooms and on the practice field. But they are also relieved that their pro careers are finally starting. Many have fulfilled dreams and life goals that developed when they were small children.

A mentor can help a rookie make the leap from college to pro. Peterson was lucky. He was helped by Vikings fullback Tony Richardson, a 13-year NFL veteran, who got to know Peterson well. Richardson was impressed, telling Thayer Evans, "He's just an incredible talent. . . . He's got unique ability." Stephen Currie wrote that Richardson said, "You just pretty much tell him what to do and how to go do it, and he goes out there and does it full speed."

One of the most important skills Peterson had to work on during his first training camp was pass protection. In college, he was rarely used as a blocker to protect his quarterback. The NFL was different. In addition, Peterson had many pass routes to learn—he was now a receiver as well as a running back. He also had to develop his footwork. He had to be able to run to the spot where the blocks were forming—he had to be exactly in sync with his new offensive line. Peterson told *Minneapolis Star Tribune* writer Judd Zulgad, "Man, this is the most football I've learned since I've been playing."

Football reporter Peter King visited the Mankato camp on August 8, 2007, and wrote that he too was impressed with Peterson. He reported on "Inside the NFL" at SI.com: "I think the strongest handshake in the NFL belongs to first-round running back Adrian Peterson. . . . I had to check to see if my fingers were still attached." Nelson had always taught his son that a firm handshake was important.

Peterson was proving to be fan-friendly. He spent hours signing autographs, a task many players avoid. He remembered what it was like to be a fan. Zulgad reported: "Some top-flight running backs seem sullen and withdrawn. Peterson frequently wears a big smile."

LIVING IN EDEN PRAIRIE

When training camp ended, Peterson moved into a new home, in the rolling hills of Eden Prairie, Minnesota, near the Vikings headquarters and practice facility. He had never lived in a big house, and he wanted that dream to come true as well. *New York Times* reporter Thayer Evans visited Peterson in his new five-bedroom home.

Peterson shared the home with his half-brother Derrick (one of Nelson's sons by his first marriage). Derrick Peterson told Evans that the money had not changed Adrian. He still ate sardines, Vienna sausages, Spam, and ramen noodles. "He's still country. He's keeping it real."

The brothers tried to make the house comfortable and laid-back. The basement was painted Viking purple with a black ceiling and had a billiards table and video games. One of the bedrooms upstairs was painted lime green with blue clouds on the ceiling. It was daughter Ade'ja's room when she visited from Texas. The room had twin beds and a closet full of toys.

Soon after he bought the house, two busloads of Vikings and friends of offensive lineman Bryant McKinnie arrived at his house to celebrate McKinnie's birthday. Peterson told Kevin Seifert, "I was a little surprised, but I set the ground rules." The house survived.

THE 2007 PRESEASON

The Vikings played four preseason games in 2007. The first was on August 10 against the St. Louis Rams. Peterson made his first professional carries, for 33 yards. The next game was against the New York Jets at Giants Stadium on August 17. The NFL got an early taste of Peterson's talent.

On one play, Jet cornerback Andre Dyson closed in on Peterson to make a violent tackle. He had Peterson where he wanted him and would welcome the highly paid rookie to the NFL with a big hit. Instead, Peterson stopped and spun around, making Dyson almost lose his footwear. Peterson left Dyson clutching at thin air. Bieniemy later called the move impressive, but he was even more impressed that Peterson had been patient at the beginning of the play. He waited for his blocks to develop and did everything the coaches asked him to do. At the end of the run, Peterson lowered his shoulder into defender David Barrett, showing that he was not just fast and elusive but also powerful. Peterson took it to the house, scoring on the 43-yard run. Suddenly, many Vikings players and fans realized that Peterson might even be better than they thought. He gained 70 yards and helped lead the team to a 37-20 win.

He fit right into the team. The running backs coach told Zulgad, "He's not caught up in the fact that [he was the] seventh pick of the draft. He's still an innocent kid from Palestine, Texas, who enjoys playing football and wants to prove that he can play this game at a high level."

HIS FIRST NFL REGULAR SEASON BEGINS

The Vikings had an experienced running back, Chester Taylor, who had joined the team a year before. Given how impressive Peterson had been in the preseason, the plan was to have Taylor and Peterson share the running duties. Viking quarterback Tarvaris Jackson was young and inexperienced, so a strong running game was going to be important if the Vikings were to have success.

The Atlanta Falcons came to the Metrodome on September 9 for the 2007 regular-season opener. The first play came to Peterson: He caught the opening kickoff and ran it back 22 yards. He was off to a good start. Early in the game, Taylor injured his hip and Peterson had to take over. He gained 29 yards on four carries during the Vikings' second possession. He ran hard and was tackled hard.

The game remained close for three quarters. Early in the fourth quarter, Jackson went back to pass and was pressured by Falcon DeAngelo Hall. The pass was off target, but Peterson made an amazing off-balance catch and took off toward the end zone. He was so quick, no one even touched him: Peterson scored after sprinting 60 yards. He put the Vikings ahead for good.

He also helped his team in a way that is hard to measure: Center Matt Birk made a bad snap, and Peterson dove on the ball at his 31-yard line to recover it. If he hadn't reacted fast enough and been willing to sacrifice his body in the mad scramble, the game might have changed dramatically for the Falcons. Instead, the Vikings won 24-3. Afterward, Hall said that Peterson had hit tacklers hard for the entire game. He had made a good first impression—gaining 103 yards on 19 carries.

The Vikings, however, lost their next three games—all of them were close. The offense had not yet fully come together. Successful NFL teams almost always have a balanced attack, mixing passes and runs. With their inexperienced quarterback, though, the Vikings were not balanced: Peterson gained 108 yards in the first half against the Green Bay Packers on September 30, but had only two carries in the second half. The Vikings got behind and needed to pass more, but their passing offense was not working well. Their defense, too, was inconsistent, unable to stop teams when it needed to. The team lost again and again despite its new sensational runner.

RUNNING WILD AGAINST THE BEARS

The Vikings went to Soldier Field in Chicago on October 14 to play a crucial game against the Bears. They needed to stop their three-game losing streak. The coaches decided to let Peterson loose. He ran wild.

Tony Richardson (49) and Peterson celebrate Peterson's 60-yard touchdown pass against the Atlanta Falcons in 2007. The pass was even more extraordinary because it occurred during Peterson's first regular season NFL game.

In the second quarter, Peterson started left on one play, made a cut at midfield, ran through a tackler, and headed for the end zone. No one caught him once he was in his cruise phase. That 67-yard touchdown run was followed later by an even more remarkable play: Peterson got the ball and headed to the right side of the line, ran through a hole in the defensive wall, cut left, put on a burst of speed, and got into a race to the end zone with Bears cornerback Charles Tillman. Peterson doesn't lose those races. He scored a 73-yard touchdown.

Late in the fourth quarter, he somehow avoided being knocked out of bounds by three Bears as he sprinted down the right sideline. He scored a 35-yard touchdown. The Bears, though, fought back, and the game was tied, 31-31, with only seconds to go. The Vikings needed one more heroic play: Peterson ran back a kickoff 53 yards. Ryan Longwell then kicked a career-long 55-yard field goal as time ran out. The Vikings won, 34-31. Peterson had run for 224 yards on 20 carries. That broke the Vikings' single-game rushing record of 200. And no one on any team had ever run for that many yards against the Bears.

What meant even more to his team was that he gained 361 all-purpose yards, the third-highest total in NFL history for a single game. His extraordinary performance made the entire league take notice. ESPN and the NFL Channel now devoted more time to his highlights. He was a force in the NFL in only his fifth game. But more records were about to fall.

THE BEST DAY EVER

When the San Diego Chargers came to the Metrodome on November 4, they were favored to win. They had one of the best run defenses in the league, had twice as many wins as the Vikings, and had not lost a November game for several years. They also had the most feared running back in the NFL other than Peterson, LaDainian Tomlinson.

By now, the league knew who Peterson was, and it knew the Viking passing offense was weaker than its running game. So, the Chargers "packed the box." When he left the huddle,

Peterson could count eight and nine Chargers waiting for him near the line of scrimmage. The strategy worked in the first half, and the Chargers led at halftime, 14-7. They seemed on their way to a victory.

Early in the third quarter, however, something changed. Peterson got more in sync with his offensive line in dealing with the packed box. They blocked their men away from the exact spot where he was headed. He waited for the blocks to develop, showing the patience that his coaches had emphasized. His linemen trusted that he would go where their blocks were most effective, and he trusted that his linemen would play hard the entire play, knowing that he might still be on his feet. His blockers didn't stop at one block—they carried through to anyone they could. Small holes widened into bigger ones. Running lanes developed.

And Peterson began to improve his use of subtle running techniques, using head fakes to throw off the linebackers watching his upper body to see where he was going. He pretended that he was going to one hole in the line but was really headed to another. Peterson was using not just power and speed, but deception. The combination wore down the Chargers. He made gain after gain. Then he broke free for a spectacular 64-yard touchdown run, tying the score.

With just over seven minutes to go in a close game, the Vikings had the ball on the Chargers' 46-yard line. Peterson took the handoff from quarterback Brooks Bollinger (Jackson was injured) and headed to the right side of the line to a spot where the play was designed. Tight end Jim Kleinsasser needed a split second more time to block a linebacker, and Peterson hesitated for an instant, waiting for his blocker to work. He then burst past both players, cut to the sideline, and scored the game-clinching touchdown. He gained 146 yards in the fourth quarter. He was still going strong as the game clock ticked down, and the Charger defense could not keep up with him. The defenders often had their hands on their knees between

During a game against the San Diego Chargers in his rookie season, Peterson broke the all-time NFL rushing record for a single game. Above, Peterson (28) hurdles Chargers linebacker Carlos Polk (52) as Viking guard Steve Huchinson blocks Chargers defensive tackle Ryon Bingham (97).

plays, trying to catch their breath. Peterson stood upright, not even breathing hard. The Vikings won, 35-17.

With a few seconds left in the game, Peterson made a small 3-yard gain. He did not realize that, with that run, he had broken the all-time NFL rushing record for a single game. He had rushed for 296 yards, one more than the record Jamal Lewis had set in 2003. He had made NFL history in only his eighth game.

Viking equipment managers had to guard his purple No. 28 jersey and white pants. The NFL Hall of Fame wanted them. An exhibit of his record-setting performance would be set up within a few weeks at the Canton, Ohio, facility. Peterson had never been to Canton but looked forward to going there with his family some day. He told Associated Press reporter Dave Campbell, "You just look for the future and expect bigger things to come and envision maybe one day, God's will, that I will be in the Hall of Fame itself." Another goal had been set.

BACK AT HOME

Suddenly, people beyond the pro football world wanted to know everything about this extraordinary player. Writer Jeff D'Alessio later profiled Peterson in the *Sporting News* and found that Peterson's television is usually on the NFL Network or ESPN. Peterson's iPod has Li'l Wayne, Notorious B.I.G., and Jamie Foxx. His favorite actress is Halle Berry, and his favorite athletes are Tiger Woods, LeBron James, and Kobe Bryant. His favorite part of himself is his hands, not his legs. He said that he thinks his worst habit is putting things off for another day. Peterson's goals beyond football are to travel to other countries and experience other cultures. And he wishes he could play the piano. He reiterated his motto, "No excuses."

Minneapolis Star Tribune writer Kevin Seifert visited Peterson at his Eden Prairie home during the middle of the season. Seifert wrote that several relatives were visiting from Palestine at the time. An aunt and uncle were cooking boiled cabbage, macaroni and cheese, cornbread, and sweet potato pie in the kitchen. Derrick and Adrian played pool in the basement. Seifert described the scene:

> "You better just sit back and watch what's fixing to happen here," Adrian tells a visitor.
>
> "See what I have to deal with?" Derrick says, laughing.

Dinner awaits, and the game ends early. Adrian hustles upstairs. He dreams of unprecedented professional success. But on this night, amid the happy commotion, it seems Adrian Peterson already has most of what he ever wanted.

"I look at this and realize I am truly blessed," he said.

Bonita told Seifert, "Sometimes I think all he really wants to do is just have fun with his family."

His neighbors have been known to put up good-luck signs on his and their lawns on game day. They bring him cookies and brownies. He also started to explore the area just beyond his neighborhood, going to Valleyfair and the Mall of America. His favorite place to eat is Wildfire, a steakhouse.

In early November 2007, however, it was getting colder in Minnesota. Peterson told Seifert, "When I got drafted here, that's the first crazy thought that went into my head. I'd always heard how cold it is. People tell me that 45 [degrees, the temperature on the day of the interview] is nothing. . . . To me, that is freezing." He would have to get used to his first northern winter. Receiver Terrell Owens would later tell reporters that Peterson would have to buy a lot of fur coats.

RIPPING UP A KNEE

Glory in the NFL is week to week, not forever. On November 11 at Lambeau Field against the rival Packers, Peterson's record setting temporarily came to an end. In the second half, Peterson caught a short pass and raced to the Packer 26-yard line. From his left, Packer defender Al Harris dove at Peterson's right knee. Harris hit the inside of the knee, pushing it outward. The hit tore a ligament. Peterson knew the pain that shot through his leg was a bad sign. He had known ankle and shoulder injuries in college, but this was a knee, the running back's most vulnerable joint—a knee injury for a running back is a serious problem.

That night, Peterson got little sleep. He feared the worst, a full tear of a major ligament. The next day several tests showed that the worst had not happened, but on a scale of one to three (three being the worst), he had a two-plus injury. He went into full-time rehab, making him joke to reporters that "A.D." now stood for "all day" in the training room.

NFL players, and rookies especially, have to fight through injuries as fast as they can or they may lose their job. The pressure on them to come back quickly is enormous, and Peterson put more pressure on himself than anyone. Just as he had returned early to play in the Fiesta Bowl, he came back to the lineup only three weeks later.

Peterson played against the Detroit Lions wearing a knee brace, but he did well. He gained 116 yards and scored two touchdowns. Athletes, however, know that it is often not the first game back from an injury that is important; it is the second. That game tells how much healing has taken place. Peterson's second game back was his worst as a football player at any level. The San Francisco 49ers held him to three yards on 14 carries.

He recovered slowly but never completely for the rest of the season. He managed to gain 78 yards the next week against the Bears, but could gain only 27 against the Redskins and 36 against Denver in the season's last two games. With Peterson underpowered, the Vikings did not make the play-offs and ended the year at 8–8.

TWO AWARDS FOR A "PLAYMAKER"

In his rookie season, Peterson gained 1,341 yards, second only to LaDainian Tomlinson in the NFL. As a result, he was named the Associated Press NFL Offensive Rookie of the Year. He knew that the great running backs Jim Brown, Emmitt Smith, and Eric Dickerson had also won the award. Peterson told Barry Wilner of the Associated Press, "It's a great honor to join a list with names like those. They are guys I looked up to growing up. It's a goal that I set before the year started . . . so it feels great to accomplish that." While accepting the award, Peterson said, "I am a playmaker." Everyone agreed.

He had also been voted into the Pro Bowl by fans and sportswriters, an unusual honor for a first-year player. The problem for a rookie at the Pro Bowl, however, is that veterans have a Pro Bowl tradition: Rookies are expected to pay for many food, beverage, and spa charges for the experienced players. Peterson told reporters that he was going to keep his room number secret.

THE RUNNING BACK AS GLADIATOR

Many sports reporters have made comparisons between Roman gladiators and modern American football players. Both are known for spectacular displays of controlled violence before large crowds wanting to be entertained. Roman citizens watching the gladiator games rooted for their favorites, as do American fans. And each trained gladiator had a special skill in combat, whether using a sword, a net and trident (similar to a three-pronged pitchfork), a club, or some other weapon. Similarly, football players have special skills, whether running or tackling or passing. Gladiators became known for their passion and will, which pushed them to their physical limits. Football players are similar.

Of course, gladiators were usually slaves or prisoners of war playing in games that ended in death for the loser. Many were dead men walking when they entered the arena. American football players are well paid and do not die if they lose. But there is one other point of comparison: Both performed with injuries, some of them severe.

Author Mike Freeman in *Bloody Sundays* writes that a typical running back such as Emmitt Smith has been hit thousands of times, kicked and punched a few hundred, and poked in

By the time the game was held, on February 10, 2008, in Honolulu, Hawaii, Peterson's knee was nearly healed. This was bad news for his opponents, the American Football Conference (AFC) players. Peterson's Vikings were part of the National Football Conference (NFC). All-stars from the two conferences play against each other in the Pro Bowl.

Rookies don't usually shine in the Pro Bowl. Running backs Marshall Faulk and Ricky Williams were the only two first-year players in the last 25 years who had won the Most

the eye a few dozen times. He writes that "playing the position destroys the human body, slowly." A running back has an average NFL career of 2.57 years, making some say that NFL stands for "Not For Long." Only 6 percent of running backs last 10 years, as opposed to 24 percent of offensive linemen.

Players have to draw a line between injuries that cause so much pain or damage they cannot perform and injuries that can be worked around. That line can be a blurry one. *Minneapolis Star Tribune* writer Jim Souhan summarized Adrian Peterson's injury-prone style:

> Peterson's greatness is not based on elusiveness. He'll make a defender miss with his speed and cuts in the open field, but most of his carries end with his ramming a defender and twisting awkwardly for the extra yard. What makes him admirable makes him an injury risk. . . . Peterson is built to thrill, not to last.

Gladiators thrilled but didn't last long. The ones who survived learned how to protect themselves. Peterson is learning to do the same.

Valuable Player (MVP) award for the game. Peterson was about to become the third.

The AFC was well ahead by the third quarter. Then Peterson found a small hole in the defense, bounced to the outside of the field, and ran 17 yards for a touchdown. Later, with only two minutes left, he broke to his right, then made a one-cut up the middle, and scored a second touchdown. NFC teammate Shawn Andrews wrapped him in a bear hug. The NFC won, 42-30. Peterson had run for 129 yards and scored twice. He was the first player since Marshall Faulk to gain more than 100 yards.

Peterson was awarded the MVP trophy, which comes with a brand-new red Cadillac. As he was checking out his new car in front of reporters at Aloha Stadium, he said, "Can I top this year? Oh yeah." He could indeed.

Leading
the League

All football players welcome the off-season as a chance to recover physically and mentally from the demands of the game. Running backs absorb as much or more punishment as any players, and Adrian Peterson takes more pounding than most running backs. He and his knee needed the rest.

The off-season gave him a chance to visit friends and family as well. NFL running backs are a kind of elite club, and in the summer of 2008, Peterson visited one of the club members, the New Orleans Saints' Reggie Bush. Bush and Peterson were born only 19 days apart and were always being compared as two of the best runners in the game. Peterson visited Bush's house in Los Angeles, with several of Bush's friends. Peterson told *Star Tribune* writer Chip Scoggins, "We just kicked it and had a good time for the weekend."

The off-season also gave him a chance to give back. He sponsored the Adrian Peterson Football Camp in Norman, Oklahoma, and helped pay the expenses for many young boys in Texas to attend. His new All Day Foundation gave donations to the East Texas Food Bank and helped support several other charitable organizations.

Peterson was also able to reap some rewards. He was a celebrity now, and he made many commercials. Wearing an astronaut suit, Peterson could be seen in a television ad for Vitamin Water with fellow sports superstars Dwight Howard and David Ortiz and rapper 50 Cent. Viking quarterback Tarvaris Jackson told reporters that he couldn't believe what he was seeing.

Peterson pulled a parachute while running in a Nike ad. He worked with Special Olympics athletes in a football camp. ESPN.com reported that Peterson said, "I've really been pulled in a lot of different directions this off-season, and I have to learn to say no better. . . . But it comes with the territory." His family and the Vikings' coaches knew he would not get too caught up in the glamour of being a star. But there was one day of celebration he would not have missed for the world.

ADRIAN PETERSON DAY

In late June 2008, Peterson went to Palestine to take part in "Adrian Peterson Day." *Palestine Herald-Press* writer Sally Sexton covered the event, noting that a parade through the center of town ended at the Texas State Railroad depot for speeches and honors.

Among the speakers were members of the M.O.M (Mothers on a Mission) Squad, a group of mothers of NFL players and other celebrities who want to offer positive choices for children hurt by crime, poverty, low literacy, and poor health care. Many children meeting Peterson and other pro athletes want to become pro athletes themselves. The M.O.M. Squad reminds those children that every athlete needs an attorney, a manager,

A humble player who never forgets his roots, Peterson involves himself in philanthropic work. During the off-season, he sponsors the Adrian Peterson Football Camp and often pays the expenses of underprivileged attendees. Above, Peterson talks to young participants in his camp.

and a financial adviser or accountant. Those are career opportunities better suited for most children than pro sports. Each requires literacy and education.

Palestine mayor Carolyn Salter spoke: "Adrian has been a great ambassador for our community. He has continued to respect his parents and maintained his humility." Former Dallas Cowboy Guy Brown congratulated Peterson on his accomplishments and advised him not to get too caught up in what other people think about him. Peterson himself directed a moving speech to the younger people in the crowd:

> My dad always told me to reach for the moon, because even if you fall, you will land among the stars. . . . Pray, believe, and work hard. It wasn't easy for me, and it's not going to be easy for you. But if you surround yourself with positive people, positive things will happen.

A young woman then sang "Wind Beneath My Wings," which includes the words "Did you ever know that you're my hero/and everything I would like to be?" With his mother and grandmother looking on, it had to be a special moment for the new star.

SECOND TIME AROUND: TRAINING CAMP AND PRESEASON

Peterson spent part of the off-season doing homework, watching films of the Vikings games. He knew that he had not made the best play every time in his first season, sometimes still being impatient or not running an exact pass route or missing a block. He knew he had gained only 144 yards in his last four games because of his injury and because teams were prepared for him.

When he came to training camp in Mankato for his second year, he knew he still had work to do. And he also knew what the NFL was really like: Every play counts, and many games are decided by inches, not yards.

Peterson told *Minneapolis Star Tribune* reporter Chip Scoggins that he felt more comfortable with the offense during the 2008 training camp: "I feel totally different." He impressed his coaches and teammates with his knowledge of the playbook (which has changes every year). Running backs coach Eric Bieniemy said during training camp that Peterson was "stepping up his game professionally." Viking safety Darren Sharper told Scoggins, "The guy is special. You have to come up with a better adjective than special. . . . He just has 'it.'"

Most Vikings fans agreed that Peterson had "it." When he walked onto the practice field during the 2008 camp, chants of "Adrian, Adrian" or "A.D., A.D." could be heard. ESPN.com reported that, whenever fans saw him, he instantly turned "a sleepy summer day in this southern Minnesota college town into a full-blown rock concert." He tried to sign as many autographs as he could and handled the attention with his famous smile. He was still generous with his time with fans and the media, something that cannot be said for many newly formed superstars.

Peterson always set goals at the beginning of any season, both personal goals and team goals. His personal goal for 2008 was to gain 2,000 yards and be the league's Most Valuable Player (MVP). His team goals were to win the NFC North Division and get to the Super Bowl. Viking coach Brad Childress told Scoggins, "[Peterson's] a guy that sets outrageous goals and meets them . . . and he knows he's not going to sneak up on anybody."

The Vikings lost three of their four 2008 preseason games, but they knew their team was ready to challenge for the NFC North championship. Their first test was against their archrival, the Packers.

A ROUGH START GETS SMOOTHER

The game was at Lambeau Field in Green Bay and was broadcast on *Monday Night Football*. The Packers, as usual, packed the box against Peterson, but the Vikings kept trying to run—they gained only six passing yards in the first half, scoring only 3 points. For their star running back, it was famine, famine, but no feast at first. But he kept butting his head against the Packers' defensive wall and eventually gained 103 yards. Still, it was not enough: The Vikings lost to their nemesis, 24-19.

The next game was against the Indianapolis Colts at the Metrodome, and again the Vikings had trouble scoring touchdowns. Peterson ran for 160 yards, but the Vikings lost 18-15. The passing offense was struggling, and chants of "Fire Childress" were mixed in with the Viking horns and other noises circling around the Metrodome. Peterson injured his hamstring muscle during the game but had to keep playing. The team needed him, and he had goals to accomplish. But he was not 100 percent for some time.

Childress and his staff decided to make a change at quarterback, bringing in veteran Gus Frerotte to replace Tarvaris Jackson. The offense simply needed more balance between running and passing. The move worked, and the Vikings won three of their next four games. Frerotte passed to receiver Bernard Berrian more, which took some of the pressure off Peterson. Berrian made several key touchdown catches.

The game against the New Orleans Saints on October 6, 2008, was a good example of the Vikings' more balanced approach. When the Saints defense put eight and nine men on the line of scrimmage to stop Peterson, Frerotte threw to Berrian, once for a 36-yard gain and once for a 33-yard touchdown. The quarterback told Judd Zulgad, "I know Adrian is great, but when they got nine guys in the box, it's hard to run it." Peterson gained only 32 yards on 21 carries, but with the Saints defense so concerned about him, they gave up some big pass plays. The Vikings won a tough game, 30-27. Peterson helped even when he didn't run for many yards.

GOING ON A WINNING STREAK

The 2008 Vikings defense was good and helped keep the team in many games. After the crucial November 9 victory over the Green Bay Packers, when Peterson gained 192 yards, the team went to Raymond James Stadium to play the Tampa Bay Buccaneers on November 16. The Bucs' plan was to hit Peterson hard and to plug up any gaps in their defensive wall, a strategy known as "gap control." They wanted to deny him any lanes to run in, trap him, and batter him. It was a brutal strategy, but

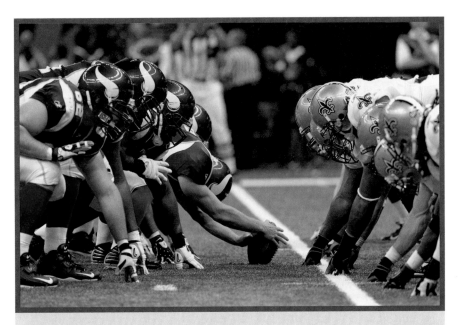

In the Vikings' game against the New Orleans Saints in October 2008, the Saints put a disproportionate number of players on their line of scrimmage on Peterson. The coverage proved how much of a threat Peterson was perceived to be.

it worked: The Bucs won, 19-13. Football expert Peter King wrote on SI.com that "gap control is far and away the most important single factor in stopping him [Peterson] from running wild."

The following week, Childress held Peterson out of practice some of the time, saying Peterson had taken so many hard hits that he needed rest. The running back, though, was also using some innovative rehab machines: A company had given him an underwater treadmill in exchange for making an appearance, and Peterson donated the machine to the Vikings so that others could benefit from it as well. The machine is used to reduce wear and tear on shins and joints as the rest of the body is being exercised or healed.

The Vikings beat the Jacksonville Jaguars on November 23, 30-12. Peterson sealed the win with a 16-yard touchdown run with 6:55 remaining in the game. He had not played the first two series in the game, however, a punishment for being late to a team meeting. He did not complain and went along with the rules that Childress had laid down—anyone late to a meeting would lose playing time.

Minnesota next played a key game against the Chicago Bears on November 30. First place in the NFC North was at stake. The game turned when the Viking defense stopped the Bears on four straight plays near the goal line. When the Vikings took over possession, most people assumed that Peterson would be given the ball to run out of danger. Instead, Frerotte threw a pass to Berrian along the sideline, and the receiver ran 99 yards for a touchdown, the longest play in Viking history. Peterson ran for 131 yards on 28 carries, including a 59-yard run. The Vikings won, 34-14. After the game, Peterson told ESPN.com: "When you have a balanced offense, it's wonderful. Especially for a running back." The team was now 7–5 and on top of the NFC North.

After beating the Detroit Lions (everyone beat the Lions in 2008), the Vikings carried a three-game winning streak into a key game against the Arizona Cardinals at University of Phoenix Stadium on December 14. This was a Cardinal team that would land in the Super Bowl a few weeks later. Childress told the team to notice how many purple jerseys were in the stands—many people from Minnesota retire to Arizona. It was almost like a home game. The Vikings' balanced attack continued: Berrian scored the first two touchdowns. On a key play with the ball deep in their own territory and 20 yards to go for a first down, Peterson broke through the line, found a hole, made a cut, and ran 32 yards. That play started a long drive that helped the Vikings win, 35-14. Peterson gained 165 yards on 28 carries and set a record: He had now rushed for more than 100 yards in nine games that season, something no other Viking had ever accomplished. Chip Scoggins wrote about Peterson that day:

Peterson's wrecking ball style and Houdini escapes have created a mutual admiration society that includes not only fans but some of the game's greatest running backs. . . . "He's the best running back in the National Football League today," Emmitt Smith said. "Right now he's the best back in the league," Eric Dickerson said. "LaDainian Tomlinson held that title for a long time. But right now [Peterson's] the guy everybody's talking about."

Smith went on to say that he appreciated Peterson's "sheer will" style of running: "He gives every ounce of himself on every run." Tacklers had to exert great force in getting Peterson down. When Scoggins told Peterson of the comments made by the other great runners, Peterson said, "I know I've been blessed, but I set goals to be the best that's ever played the game. . . . To hear those guys say those things makes me even more determined to go out and accomplish those things."

WINNING THE DIVISION

Peterson took time out from the hectic football season to surprise some kids from a Boys and Girls Club in the area. He arranged for them to be brought to Dick's Sporting Goods in Richfield, Minnesota, and given $300 each to spend. He told the Associated Press, "Growing up and not being able to have everything I wanted, I understand where a lot of these kids might be coming from." The kids were delighted, to say the least.

The four-game winning streak put the Vikings in position to win their first NFC North title since 2000. They hit a bump in the road, however, when they played the Atlanta Falcons on December 21 in the Metrodome. Teams had developed another strategy to try to stop Peterson, other than gap control. They began to try to strip him of the ball, making him fumble. Since he was such a determined runner who fought for every yard, he sometimes left himself open to having the ball punched out of his grasp. Running backs are supposed to hold the ball "high and tight." But a runner like Peterson will sometimes swing the ball away from his body to keep his balance while making a cut

HOW MUCH FORCE DOES IT TAKE TO STOP ADRIAN PETERSON?

Football players, like everybody and everything else, obey the laws of physics. Whether it is a car crash or a collision on the football field between a runner and a tackler, the rules are the same. Author Timothy Gay in *The Physics of Football* writes that the most basic law that applies to crashes and collisions is called Newton's Second Law of Motion, which says that force is equal to mass multiplied by acceleration.

Adrian Peterson runs at a top velocity of about 10 yards (9 meters)/second. His mass is 220 pounds (100 kilograms). If a tackler hits him head on, Peterson goes from 10 yards/second to 0 yards/second in about one-fifth of a second. The math doesn't lie: The force required to stop Peterson is just over 1,000 pounds (454 kilograms). That's more than half a ton, about what a small killer whale weighs.

One of the NFL's not-so-well-kept secrets is that both the runner and the tackler often try to accelerate at the last instant to increase their force at impact. Each wants to be the hammer, not the nail.

The average NFL lineman's or linebacker's mass (weight) has increased over 50 percent in the last 60 years. Their speed has also increased. So, the forces are building. They are much greater than they used to be. Without advances in helmets and pads, someone might die each month in the NFL just from the crash impacts.

or lunging for an extra yard. As a result, he had fumbled twice in his last three games, and six times for the season, more than any other running back. Defenders became like sharks going after bait.

Against Atlanta, he fumbled two more times. That helped the Falcons win, 24-17. After the game, Peterson told a group of reporters, "I'm very disappointed in my performance." He told writer Chip Scoggins that he knew he had to be "more aware that guys are going to be hitting you until you fall all the way to the ground." It always takes Peterson a day or two to get over a bad game. His coaches, though, believed in him. Childress told Scoggins, "He's an elite-caliber athlete. There are bumps in everybody's road. . . . He's a big part of what we do so we can't let him get down."

The final regular-season game was against the New York Giants at the Metrodome on December 28. If the Vikings won, they would be the NFC North champs. Early in the game, Peterson took a handoff from quarterback Tarvaris Jackson (Gus Frerotte had been injured in an earlier game) and timed his run perfectly so that a block by his right tackle sprung him free. No one touched him as he raced 67 yards for a touchdown. It was his longest run of the season, and one of his most important. The Vikings led 10-0.

The Giants came back to take the lead. On a crucial play in the fourth quarter, Peterson took a pitch, made one man miss him, spun twice to get out of the hands of two others, and leaped for a first down. The game's last play came with Viking kicker Ryan Longwell making a 50-yard field goal to win the game, 20-19. The Vikings had captured the NFC North championship. Many Vikings, including their star running back, who had gained 103 yards, put on gray caps that said they were division champs.

For the season, Peterson had rushed for 1,760 yards, more than any other running back. He had 10 100-yard games and 20 runs of more than 20 yards, the most in the NFL. He became only the fifth player in NFL history to gain more than 3,000 yards in his first two seasons. Eric Dickerson, Edgerrin James, Earl Campbell, and Clinton Portis were the other four.

SOARING AGAINST THE EAGLES, AND THEN CRASHING

The Vikings played the Philadelphia Eagles in the first weekend of the play-offs, on January 5, 2009. More than 60,000 Vikings fans packed the Metrodome and created their usual deafening noise. They were delighted to be attending their first play-off game in eight years. Outside it was near zero degrees, but inside it was carnival time.

The Eagles had a strong defense, one of the best in the NFL. They knew about gap control and hard hitting. On his first two runs, Peterson lost one yard. On his third run, he gained three. Eagle defender Brian Dawkins gave him such a hard helmet-to-helmet hit that Peterson hit the ground and lay there. The medical staff rushed to him. He had to leave the game for several plays, but, like a gladiator, he returned.

On a key play in the second quarter, on a third-and-two (two yards needed for a first down), Peterson took the handoff from Jackson. He broke through the middle of the line and cut left, but he was so fast he nearly collided with an official. He recovered and outran several Eagles to the end zone for a 40-yard touchdown run. It was the longest scoring run in Viking play-off history. He scored again in the quarter, a tough three-yard run to the left and into the end zone with Eagles all over him.

Tarvaris Jackson, though, was also in his first play-off game, and his inexperience showed. He was intercepted by Asante Samuel, who ran for a touchdown. At halftime, the Eagles led, 16-14.

In the second half, the Eagle defense held Peterson to only 17 yards, and Jackson and Berrian were not able to get the passing game going. Jackson missed on seven passes in a

In the Vikings quest to become NFC North champs in the 2008 season, Peterson ran 67 yards for a touchdown against the New York Giants. After a close game, the Vikings pulled it out. Above, Peterson celebrates the victory in the stands of the Metrodome.

row in the fourth quarter. He was blitzed again and again. In contrast, Eagles quarterback Donovan McNabb had a good day, getting better as the game went on, passing for 300 yards.

The roar of the crowd didn't seem to bother him. After a short pass to Brian Westbrook turned into a 71-yard scoring play, the Eagles pulled away and won, 26-14. Peterson had run for two touchdowns and 83 yards, but the balanced attack fell apart for the Vikings.

After the game, reporters saw Peterson sitting in front of his locker in full uniform, staring blankly. Most of his team-mates were gone. He was devastated. He told them, "It hurts. I'm hurting right now." But he and his team would learn from the experience of being in the play-offs.

ENDING THE SEASON WITH AWARDS

The end of the NFL regular season always brings a host of awards. The most prestigious is the Most Valuable Player award, voted on by 50 sportswriters and broadcasters. For 2008, Colts quarterback Peyton Manning won for the third time. Peterson tied for fourth, disappointing many Vikings fans.

But he won the Bert Bell Award, another prestigious trophy, given to the NFL's most outstanding player by the Maxwell Football Club, an exclusive club formed some 70 years earlier and named after a former NFL commissioner. Peterson also tied for second with Peyton Manning for NFL Offensive Player of the Year, an award Saints quarterback Drew Brees won.

So, for the 2008 season, he had not met his two personal goals but had come close. He had met one of his team goals, winning the division. Now, he needed his Vikings to get to the Super Bowl. Only time would tell if their offense would be balanced enough and their defense strong enough.

Peterson went to his second straight Pro Bowl in Hawaii. During his week in paradise, he often drank water when others drank heavily at the bar. One day at practice, Nelson Peterson wore a T-shirt with his son's name and number. He told reporters, "I taught him to work hard to accomplish these things in life. . . . That's what I think puts him above the rest." Drew Brees told Associated Press reporters, "He's just a phenomenal talent. I'm just glad he's on my team."

Peterson scored on a 10-yard touchdown run, and the NFC won the game, 30-21. With his last carry, the season was now over. He had done better in 2008 than in 2007. But he could not wait for 2009.

He Is
Legend

Adrian Peterson did fewer appearances and commercials in the off-season than he did the previous year. He realized that he had to protect his time more and use it to prepare for the upcoming season. He told reporters, "I've really cut back a lot this year [spring and summer of 2009]. I have more time to study film and really just focus on the most important things."

Palestine honored him with another Adrian Peterson Day in June, complete with live music and games for children. He wanted to use the event to help families in need, so he and his Adrian Peterson All Day Foundation joined with Feed the Children volunteers and local churches to hand out boxes of food to about 400 families in the area. Each box held enough food to feed a family of four for about a week. As one mother came up to him for help, Peterson noticed that a small boy with her was shy and hanging back. He knelt down and talked to the boy, who said hello in a timid voice. Peterson put the boy at ease. Associated Press reporter Scott Tyler wrote that the moment "will be a memory the young Peterson fan will have for a long time."

During the off-season, NFL Films sent a crew to film Peterson in his everyday activities. The company was producing a DVD about him. He was now one of the NFL's most popular players.

About 400 kids came to his football camp in Norman during the summer. He even played quarterback for them, throwing passes and showing them how to avoid blitzes. No one, however, expects Peterson to become a quarterback anytime soon.

GIVING THE OFFENSE MORE BALANCE

The Vikings had ranked no higher than twenty-fifth in the NFL in passing during Peterson's first two years. As a result, teams were still packing the box against him and giving him more famine than feast on most plays. Other than Bernard Berrian, opponents really feared only Peterson and planned many ways to stop him.

The Vikings had two ways to solve the problem of having teams focus only on Peterson. The first solution was to sign an experienced and proven quarterback who could improve the passing game. So, they signed Brett Favre, the former Packer and Jet quarterback who would certainly be a Hall of Famer. Favre was still in his late thirties and seemed to have at least another year of great play left in him. Peterson had watched Favre growing up and admired his passion. He welcomed him to the team.

The second solution was to draft a speedy and elusive receiver who could also line up in the backfield. Such a player could take some of the pressure off Peterson and force teams to plan for another runner. So, the Vikings drafted Percy Harvin, who had electrified Florida Gator fans for the past three years.

The Wildcat offense had come into the NFL in 2008: In it, a back receives the ball directly from the center, standing some five to seven yards behind him. Harvin could be used as a back for that offense in addition to many other roles, including catching passes and returning kicks.

Chip Scoggins wrote that Peterson met Harvin for the first time in May at an Organized Team Activity (OTA, an off-season practice session). Harvin recalled, "All he said was to come out here and work hard. He said play fast even if you don't know something. Play 100 miles per hour and eventually the coaches will catch you up." It was on-the-job training, NFL-style.

CONTINUING TO IMPROVE

Vikings running backs coach Eric Bieniemy told reporters in May 2009 that he "thought [Peterson] made a tremendous jump from [his rookie season], but also I think he will improve again this year." He pointed out that Peterson had four fumbles in 2007 but nine in 2008, the most in the NFL. Working on avoiding fumbles became an emphasis during training camp in 2009.

Peterson, however, was also getting tired of people pointing out this problem. He told Kevin Seifert in August, "I was thinking about it [fumbling] too much and I got caught up in it. . . . I've been doing this since I was seven. I know how to hold onto the ball."

He reported to training camp at 220 pounds (100 kg). He was measured as having 6 percent body fat, a very low percentage. Fit male athletes range from 6 to 13 percent body fat. The only people with a lower fat content are trained bodybuilders, who try to come to a meet with only 3 to 4 percent. He had talked in the off-season about gaining 10 pounds (4.5 kg) and reporting at 230 (104 kg), but that did not happen.

Peterson and his quarterback, Brett Favre (4), celebrate after Favre throws a touchdown against the Green Bay Packers in 2009. Favre was signed to increase the passing game and take the pressure off Peterson.

Another emphasis in training camp was to run more precise pass routes and do better pass blocking. During the preseason, Brad Childress and the Viking coaches did not want to risk getting Peterson hurt, so he did not play much. But when he did, he reminded fans what happens when he is healthy and rested. On the first play of a preseason game on August 31, 2009, against the Houston Texans, he took a handoff from Favre, ran through a hole in the right side of the line, and sprinted 75 yards down the right side of the field for a touchdown. Favre had never had this kind of runner in his offense before. He celebrated with Peterson in the Texan end zone.

A REVEALING INTERVIEW

Sporting News writer Steve Greenberg conducted a famous interview with Peterson and legendary running back Jim Brown before the 2009 season began. The interview took place in Brown's Los Angeles home and began with Brown telling Peterson: "I have great admiration for you and your ability." Peterson responded that he thought Brown was "the best football player to play the game." Brown asked several questions, and said, "The territory that we're in now, only running backs understand these questions. People think coaches are always right, but it's difficult to teach a runner how to run, because every runner is different." Brown added that it was also difficult to teach a runner what to do at the moment of impact, the time when both the runner and the tackler try to win a one-on-one struggle that is sometimes hidden from view.

Brown asked Peterson, "Have you ever had a 10-yard run that was better than a 60-yard run?" Peterson answered that he had. He remembered one play in college when the Sooners had the ball on the other team's 8-yard line and Peterson ran with his "shoulders low, just driving, breaking tackles. When I watched that play again, I was like, 'Man, I was determined to get into the end zone.'"

Brown analyzed Peterson's running: "Your ability to make moves on the move, to accelerate, to break tackles, is what makes you special. . . . That speed is a big deal, let's be honest. I call it the fourth gear. You know you have it." Brown watches NFL running backs and has an insider's knowledge of them. He said Peterson gets more yards than he should on many plays. Several other backs get less than they should. Peterson said he often thought he should have gained more yards on a certain play: "I should've broken that tackle!"

Peterson told Brown that he is a religious man. "You can do all things through God, and He'll never put more on you than you can bear. Those are the two things I've fallen back on. With my dad being gone, as bad as that was, God never gives you more than you can handle."

In the course of the interview, they talked about some of the great running backs of all time. They agreed that Gale Sayers was one of the greatest runners, as was Earl Campbell. Brown asked Peterson whether he had ever heard of Ollie Matson. Peterson said no. Brown replied, "The Rams traded nine men to get him [from the Chicago Cardinals in 1959], and he was an Olympic sprinter and one of the all-time greats, but very few people would probably know him." Peterson said he admired several backs now playing, including LaDainian Tomlinson, Maurice Jones-Drew, and Brandon Jacobs.

DEFINING ATHLETIC GENIUS

The interview with Brown raised a number of points about why Peterson is an athletic genius. Often the best athletes do not have the highest SAT or IQ scores. They instead possess a different kind of intelligence, one that is hard for them to put into words. Athletes as great as Peterson and Brown have a way of taking a great deal of visual information into their brains and turning that into an instant physical reaction by their nervous systems and muscles. Sports psychologists call this "speed and span of recognition." Players are making instinctive and quick decisions but are still drawing on their memories and their will. They are thinking without thinking, reacting in the blink of an eye. The player and the play become one thing. They are not distracted by the crowd or anything else.

Some sports make more demands than others—baseball, basketball, and football are complicated, with many sources of visual information. Golf and tennis, for example, have fewer

WHO IS CONSIDERED THE BEST RUNNING BACK OF ALL TIME?

Sports people love to make lists, and listing the best NFL running backs of all time always grabs attention. List-makers note that the back who gains the most yards is not necessarily the greatest runner. Emmitt Smith's 18,355 career yards gained are the most ever, but few put Smith at the top because his offensive line was so good. The best must not only be able to excel in gaining yards, receiving passes, and blocking, but they also need other strengths: durability and the ability to play well in pain. And they need to lead.

So, different people have come up with different rankings. The following table is a sample, showing the rankings from a football reference site, a blogger (Bofah), and a book writer (Freeman).

RANK	PRO-FOOTBALLREFERENCE.COM	KOFI BOFAH	MIKE FREEMAN
1	Jim Brown	Jim Brown	Jim Brown
2	Marshall Faulk	Walter Payton	Gale Sayers
3	Barry Sanders	Emmitt Smith	O.J. Simpson
4	Walter Payton	Thurman Thomas	Eric Dickerson
5	LaDainian Tomlinson	Barry Sanders	Barry Sanders
6	Emmitt Smith	Tony Dorsett	Marshall Faulk
7	Eric Dickerson	Eric Dickerson	Walter Payton
8	Curtis Martin	LaDainian Tomlinson	Emmitt Smith
9	Thurman Thomas	O.J. Simpson	Earl Campbell
10	Edgerrin James	Gale Sayers	Tony Dorsett

sources of visual information (no or only one opponent to keep track of). No sport makes more information-processing demands than football.

Most lists have Jim Brown at the top. He was simply faster and more powerful than almost all of his tacklers, and his 5.2 yards per carry is the highest for an NFL career of more than five years. He never missed a game and made the Pro Bowl every year he played. Mike Freeman writes in *Bloody Sundays*, "Brown is the most physically sturdy, mentally tough, and versatile athlete the NFL has ever seen."

Walter Payton had legendary durability, speed, and power. He was so tough he sometimes got a penalty for the way he treated tacklers. Like Adrian Peterson, he hated to run out of bounds without delivering a hit. Gale Sayers was perhaps the most elusive runner in the open field in NFL history and was never caught from behind, but he played in only 68 games because of badly injured knees. Barry Sanders cut so fast and so often that a few tacklers broke or sprained their ankles trying to keep up with him. Defenders said they attacked other runners, but only tried to wait in gangs for Sanders to come to them. They just hoped to contain him. Emmitt Smith has the most yards for a career and was perhaps the most durable back in history. No one hit the hole faster than Eric Dickerson, and he still holds the record for most yards in a season (2,105 in 1984).

Peterson is a combination of several of these great runners. With Brown's strength and toughness, Sayers's elusiveness, and Dickerson's ability to hit the hole fast, he has dazzled the NFL in his first years. If he meets all his goals, he might even replace Jim Brown at the top.

So when a Jim Brown or an Adrian Peterson "reads" a defense, he is making interpretations and decisions at light-speed. He has to see which of his blockers is winning and losing and react to that information. If his right tackle is winning and has the left defensive end moving ever so slightly to the outside, he has to cut inside. If the left defensive end is leaning to the inside of the field, he will cut outside and then decide how to handle the linebacker moving into position. Another series of decisions starts. And another begins when the safety comes up.

Speed, power, quickness, and sheer will are not enough for an athletic genius. His or her ability to see, read, and react is also needed. Each great back in the NFL, and each great world athlete, has that genius.

THE 2009 SEASON BEGINS

The Vikings opened their 2009 season on September 13, against the Cleveland Browns. With six minutes to go, the Vikings had the ball on their 36-yard line. Favre handed off to Peterson, who burst through a hole in the left side created by his linemen Bryant McKinnie and Steve Hutchinson. He juked (faked a move one way and went another) the safety and cut left. He ran over one tackler and sidestepped another. He then stopped, pushed one defender to the ground with his right arm, and accelerated down the left sideline so fast that he was pulling away from everyone after 10 yards. Peterson scored a 64-yard touchdown and put the game away. He gained 180 yards on 25 carries and scored three touchdowns. The Vikings won, 34-20.

The Vikings were tied with the Detroit Lions on September 20 midway through the third quarter when Peterson broke into the clear at the Lions' 27 and ran in for a touchdown, the first time the Vikings led all day. Brett Favre threw two touchdown passes, one to rookie Percy Harvin. The Viking offense had the balance it needed to win, 27-13.

One of the most anticipated games of the early part of the 2009 season was played on October 5. The great Minnesota-Wisconsin rivalry was onstage, as Viking quarterback Brett Favre faced his old Packer team in the Metrodome. *Monday Night Football* announcers Ron Jaworski, Jon Gruden, and Mike Tirico talked about how the crowd felt "electric" before the game.

The new balance in the Viking offense continued to work well. As the Packers concentrated only on stopping Peterson, Favre threw three touchdown passes. Several Packers often followed Peterson wherever he went, so other Vikings could make plays. Peterson finished with only 55 yards on 25 carries, and he was stripped of the ball by rookie Clay Matthews, but the Vikings won, 30-23. The team was now 4–0 and the talk of the league.

THE 2009 SEASON: SO NEAR, YET SO FAR

The new Vikings with Favre, Harvin, and a ferocious defense dominated and won the NFC North in 2009. With the new players, Peterson's role changed. He caught many more passes than ever before (43), but he was also often used as a decoy, a way of distracting defenses while Favre picked them apart with passes. Peterson still gained 1,383 yards, fifth best in the league, and he was a touchdown-scoring machine with a league-leading 18. He was again selected to play in the Pro Bowl.

On January 17, 2010, Peterson was matched in a play-off game against the team he loved as a child, the Dallas Cowboys. The Viking defense showed no mercy as it raided the Cowboy passing game, sacking quarterback Tony Romo six times and making him fumble away his team's chances. Favre threw for four touchdowns, and the Vikings won 34-3.

The next game was the most important one of Peterson's life. On Sunday evening, January 24, 2010, the Vikings faced the New Orleans Saints in the Louisiana Superdome for the

NFC championship, the game that decides one of the two Super Bowl teams. On the first possession, Peterson scored a 19-yard touchdown on a run that inspired his team. He took a handoff from Favre, accelerated explosively through the Saints defensive line, cut left, and was gone.

Like two mixed-martial-arts combatants, the teams fought with everything they had for 60 minutes and were tied at the end of regulation. Peterson had done well, scoring two more touchdowns on punishing short runs that showed both his strength and his will. He ran for 122 yards, only the fourth time he had topped 100 yards all year. But he had also fumbled twice, miraculously recovering one himself some 15 yards down the field in a mad free-for-all. He later accepted responsibility for a dropped handoff from Favre, even though replays showed the quarterback never placed the ball where Peterson could clutch it. Favre later made the biggest mistake of the game and the 2009 season when he threw an interception as the Vikings were nearing game-winning field goal range with seconds left in regulation.

The Saints won the overtime coin toss, and the Vikings never got the ball back. The Saints won, 31-28, in a conference championship game considered one of the NFL's all-time best. Reporter Chip Scoggins wrote that Peterson stood in the doorway of the darkened tunnel to the locker room well after the game, watching the confetti fall on the Saints.

2010: A BRIGHT LIGHT IN A DARK SEASON

The failed hopes of the 2009 season seemed to carry over into the Vikings' 2010 season. Their first 2010 game was against the Super Bowl champions, the Saints. The city of New Orleans still seemed to be celebrating: Dave Matthews, Taylor Swift, and Brad Pitt were among the many who watched the Saints beat the Vikings again, this time in a 14-9 defensive struggle that featured the Saints holding Peterson to 87 yards and intercepting Favre again. That loss deflated the Vikings, and the team lost five of its first seven games, digging itself into

Adrian Peterson has risen above several crushing personal tragedies with hard work, a gracious attitude, and strong leadership skills. Although he has been compared to legendary running backs Jim Brown and Eric Dickerson, it is too soon to tell where Adrian Peterson will rank among the NFL's greatest.

a deep hole. The glittering 2009 season looked now like fool's gold. Brett Favre turned into a mere mortal, several receivers got hurt, and the defense was not overpowering.

Peterson, however, was a bright light in a dark season: He gained more than 130 yards in each of several early games, against the Dolphins, the Lions, and the dreaded Packers, and he ended the year with 1,298 yards. He single-handedly ignited the offense in several games: The Vikings were losing 24-10 at the Metrodome to the Arizona Cardinals on November 7 with just over three minutes left when Peterson took over the game with heart and attitude. He launched himself into the end zone for one touchdown and later dragged several Cardinals on his way to a long run setting up another touchdown. The Vikings tied the game and won in overtime.

On December 28 in Philadelphia, the Eagles were expected to beat the Vikings easily. Favre had been injured with a concussion, and Peterson had an ankle injury and a painful thigh bruise that made walking, let alone running, difficult. But the show went on. In one key play, rookie quarterback Joe Webb handed off to Peterson at the Eagles' 33-yard line, and the running back headed right, cut left at the line, and went 27 yards before being tackled by three players. Two plays later, he headed toward the end zone and faced four Eagles. He somehow submarined his way past them and scored. The Vikings won, 24-14.

The ESPN announcers noted that Peterson had 20 fumbles in his first three seasons (2007–2009), the most in the NFL among non-quarterbacks, but that he had none for the 2010 season going into the Eagles game. Of course, he fumbled soon after that announcement, but he had overcome his biggest weakness. He told Kevin Seifert that he had stopped bracing himself with his football-clutching hand as he was falling to the ground, holding the ball higher and tighter and away from tacklers.

The Vikings' 2010 season was symbolized by the much-viewed collapse of the Metrodome on December 12 after a snowstorm. A small tear quickly became a gaping hole, and the avalanche that hit the field created a new and unwelcome roar in the stadium. Just a few weeks before the collapse, coach Brad Childress had been fired. As Peterson said to Kevin Seifert of ESPN, the season "hasn't gone the way we planned."

THE PETERSON LEGEND

The ups and down of the Vikings have not diminished Peterson's stature and visibility in the NFL. Nike used Peterson in a video commercial for its Pro Combat training apparel in an ad called "Trail of Destruction, Alter Ego." It features Peterson tearing through defenses unable to stop him on a dark and muddy field. Each tackle attempt is a form of mortal combat. Peterson wins each battle, twisting and fighting his way to the goal line. Being tackled seems to be a form of imprisonment, and he will not be taken prisoner. At the end, his skin turns an alien/reptilian texture, and viewers see that this is a version of Peterson, not of this world. This "alter ego" has left a trail of destruction behind him. The commercial shows his combative side, his will to avoid capture. This part of Peterson makes some defenders want to back up, wait for help, and hope to contain him.

The Nike commercial and others for Vitamin Water and NFL Mobile Redzone show how much a part of pro football he has become. He may have been born with great athletic ability, but he has worked hard to shape that ability to the demands of an NFL running back and to create a positive public image for himself. He has tried not only to achieve excellence despite any limitations or obstacles, but he has also tried to show others how to do the same. Peterson may run for a living, but he never tries to hide from responsibility. He has worked to become a good citizen of his hometown, his home state of Texas, Oklahoma, Minnesota, the NFL, and the country. Giving back to others and being respectful as well are in his nature.

Peterson's full greatness has yet to be measured. If ancient Greeks admired amazing acts of strength and swiftness, so too do modern audiences. Each game throughout the ages is a contest in an arena that produces struggle and change. Players such as Peterson cannot wait for the next game to begin.

The death and imprisonment of loved ones have helped shape his life, but he has not let those losses define his life. He may not be built to last, but he is indeed built to thrill and give his fans magic moments. Only time will tell whether he becomes the top or one of the top NFL running backs of all time. But Peterson has already accomplished so much. He has escaped being a victim of his circumstances and has succeeded in taking control of his world. He represents the dreams of small-town children everywhere, especially those who want to know that they can overcome early tragedies in their lives. He has reached for the moon and landed among the stars.

ADRIAN PETERSON

POSITION: Running back

FULL NAME: Adrian Lewis Peterson
BORN: March 21, 1985, Palestine, Texas
HEIGHT: 6'1"
WEIGHT: 217 lbs.

COLLEGE: University of Oklahoma
TEAMS: Minnesota Vikings (2007–)

YEAR	TEAM	G	ATT	YARDS	Y/C	TD	REC	YARDS	Y/R	TD
2007	MIN	14	238	1,341	5.6	12	19	268	14.1	1
2008	MIN	16	363	1,760	4.8	10	21	125	6.0	0
2009	MIN	16	314	1,383	4.4	18	43	436	10.1	0
2010	MIN	15	283	1,298	4.6	12	36	341	9.5	1
	TOTALS	**61**	**1,198**	**5,782**	**4.8**	**52**	**119**	**1,170**	**9.8**	**2**

CHRONOLOGY

1985   Adrian Peterson is born on March 21 in Palestine, Texas.

1993   Brother Brian is killed by a drunken driver.

Joins Anderson County Youth Football League.

1997   Leads his football team to the championship at a Texarkana, Texas, tournament.

1998   His father, Nelson Peterson, is arrested and sent to prison for crimes related to selling drugs.

2003   Rushes for 2,960 yards in his senior year at Palestine High.

2004   Plays in U.S. Army All-American Bowl on January 3 and scores two touchdowns.

TIMELINE

1985
Born on March 21 in Palestine, Texas

1993
Brother Brian is killed by a drunken driver

1998
His father is arrested and sent to prison

2003
Rushes for 2,960 yards as a high school senior

2004
Wins Hall Trophy as best high school football player

1985 — **2004**

Wins Hall Trophy as best high school football player.

Enters the University of Oklahoma.

Gains 225 yards in an October 9 game against the University of Texas.

Gains 249 yards in an October 30 game against Oklahoma State University.

Comes in second in voting for the Heisman Trophy.

2005   Plays in the national championship game on January 4 against University of Southern California. Oklahoma loses, 55-19.

Badly injures right ankle in an October 1 game.

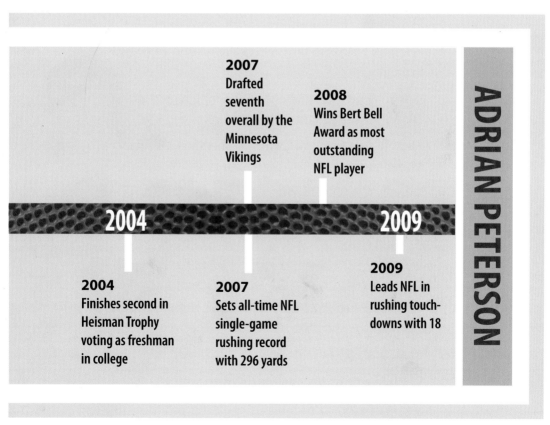

2007
Drafted seventh overall by the Minnesota Vikings

2008
Wins Bert Bell Award as most outstanding NFL player

2004

2009

2004
Finishes second in Heisman Trophy voting as freshman in college

2007
Sets all-time NFL single-game rushing record with 296 yards

2009
Leads NFL in rushing touch-downs with 18

ADRIAN PETERSON

Gains 237 yards against Oklahoma State in 42-14 win on November 26.

2006 Father is released from prison and watches Peterson in person for the first time in eight years in an October 14 game. Peterson breaks his collarbone scoring touchdown.

2007 Plays on January 1 in the Fiesta Bowl against Boise State University in one of college football's most memorable games. Oklahoma loses in overtime, 43-42.

Peterson announces on January 15 that he will enter the NFL Draft and not play his last year at Oklahoma.

Is drafted seventh overall by the Minnesota Vikings.

Signs $40.5 million contract with the Vikings.

Gains 103 yards in his first regular-season game on September 9.

Sets all-time NFL single-game rushing record with 296 yards in a game on November 4.

2008 Plays in first Pro Bowl, winning the Most Valuable Player trophy.

Vikings win NFC North.

For the 2008 season, Peterson gains 1,760 yards, to lead the league. He is only the fifth player in NFL history to rush for more than 3,000 yards in his first two seasons.

Wins Bert Bell Award for most outstanding player in the NFL.

2009 Plays in second Pro Bowl.

Leads league in rushing touchdowns with 18.

Voted into 2010 Pro Bowl.

2010   Rushes for three touchdowns in 31-28 overtime loss to Saints in NFC Championship Game on January 24.

Leads Vikings to a dramatic 27-24 overtime win on November 7 against the Arizona Cardinals.

The roof of the Metrodome collapses on December 12.

Leads Vikings to an unexpected 24-14 win over the Philadelphia Eagles on December 28, gaining 118 yards.

Voted into 2011 Pro Bowl.

GLOSSARY

American Football Conference (AFC) One of the two conferences in the National Football League, consisting of 16 teams.

balanced offense When a team runs roughly half of the time and throws the other half, its offense is said to be balanced. A truly balanced offense means that the defense has no ability to predict when an opponent's offense is going to run or pass.

blitz A defensive play in which the linebackers or defensive backs give up their normal responsibilities to run into the offensive team's backfield to disrupt the called play.

bowl game A college football game played after the regular season is over, usually on or near New Year's Day.

carry A run with the ball, also known as a rush or rushing attempt.

center The offensive player who gets the ball to the quarterback, punter, or holder at the start of each play.

Combine An annual organized tryout camp, called the National Invitational Camp, or simply "the Combine," to which the NFL invites roughly 300 of the best college players.

cornerback A defender, also called a "corner," usually at the edges of the defensive secondary whose primary responsibility is to prevent wide receivers from catching passes. The cornerback also tries to stop runs to the outside and may blitz the quarterback as well.

cut back A runner's change in direction, usually to avoid pursuit by defensive players and often in a different direction than what was called for in the play's design.

cut up A runner's change in direction to move parallel to the sidelines and directly up the field, usually as part of a designed play.

defensive back   Any player in the defensive secondary, as opposed to the defensive line or a linebacker. His primary goal is to prevent receivers from catching passes.

down   One play. Each team has four downs to gain 10 yards.

draft   The selection of collegiate players by NFL teams.

drive   A series of plays by the offensive team that begins when it gets the ball and ends when it scores or turns the ball over to the other team.

end zone   The scoring area between the goal line and the end line, bounded by the sidelines.

field goal   A three-point score made when a player kicks the ball through the opposing team's goal posts.

first down   The first play of a series of four downs. The offense has four downs to gain 10 or more yards.

fourth down   The final play of a series of four downs when the offense has to decide to try for a first down, attempt to score, or punt the ball to the opposing team.

fullback   A running back usually responsible for blocking and gaining only a few yards when running.

fumble   A loss of control of the football by any player carrying it during a live play. Either team may recover a fumble, and the recovering team gains possession of the ball.

gap control   A gap is the space between players along the line of scrimmage. Gap control is a defensive strategy to limit or fill the gaps with defensive players after the play begins, making the running back's job much more difficult.

goal line   The line at the front of the end zone. A touchdown is scored when the football breaks the plane of the front of the opposing team's goal line between the two sidelines.

handoff   The action of a player giving the ball to a teammate, as opposed to throwing the ball.

Heisman Trophy   A prestigious award presented annually by the Downtown Athletic Club to the best player in college football, as determined by votes from previous winners and many sports journalists.

holder   The player who receives the snap and places the ball upright on the ground for the kicker attempting a field goal or an extra point.

huddle   An on-field team meeting regarding the next play or plays. Usually the quarterback calls or relays the play in the offensive huddle, and the middle linebacker calls or relays the play in the defensive huddle.

interception   A pass that is caught by a defensive player.

kickoff   A kick that begins the game, the second half, the overtime period, and the series of downs after touchdowns and field goals.

linebacker   A defensive player usually lined up behind the defensive linemen and in front of the defensive secondary.

line of scrimmage   A moving imaginary line that stretches across the width of the field to the sidelines and separates the two teams before the snap.

National Football Conference (NFC)   One of two conferences in the National Football League, consisting of 16 teams.

National Football League (NFL)   The largest professional American football league, consisting of 32 teams in two conferences, each with four divisions.

offensive lineman   Offensive player lined up very near the line of scrimmage, usually a center, guard, or tackle; job is to block for runners and passers.

off-season   The period between a team's final game and the beginning of preseason training camp.

onside kick   A short kickoff made by the kicking team with the intention of recovering the ball after it has traveled at least 10 yards.

overtime   An extra period added to a game when the score is tied at the end of regulation. In college, both teams get at least one possession of the ball. In the NFL, the first team to score wins; also called sudden death.

pass   A throw from one player to another. A forward pass goes down the field, and a lateral pass (also just called a lateral) goes backward or parallel to the line of scrimmage.

pass route   The pattern made by a receiver as he gets into position to catch a pass.

penalty   A loss of yardage or downs or both by a team breaking the rules.

playbook   The entire set of plays a team uses, traditionally in a notebook format.

play-offs   Postseason games up to and including the Super Bowl. A team must either win its division or have one of the two best records in the conference to make the play-offs.

preseason   The time before the regular season during which teams train, evaluate players, and play exhibition games.

Pro Bowl   The National Football League's all-star game.

punt   A kick in which the ball is dropped and kicked after it leaves the kicker's hands. A punt usually occurs on fourth down and is designed to set the opposing team as far back as possible.

quarterback   The player who directs the offense by calling or relaying the play and then receiving the snap and initiating the run or throw.

receiver   Offensive player who catches passes, usually either a wide receiver, tight end, or running back.

running back   An offensive player, also called a "back," whose main job is to run with the football and gain yards, block for other runners or the quarterback, or catch short passes. Halfbacks, fullbacks, and tailbacks are all backs with varying assignments, skills, and positions.

sack   A tackle of the quarterback by the defense behind the line of scrimmage.

safety   A defensive player who lines up in the secondary but often deeper than the cornerbacks. A safety is also a two-point score that occurs by tackling an opposing ball carrier in his own end zone.

secondary   A defensive player who lines up behind the line-backers, or the area of the field defended by these players.

sidelines   The lines marking where the field of play ends and out of bounds begins; also the area just outside the playing field where players and coaches stand or sit when not playing.

snap   The handoff or backward throw from the center that starts a play. The snap is usually to the quarterback, punter, or kick holder.

sudden death   An overtime period in which the team that scores first wins.

Super Bowl   The National Football League's championship game.

tackle   To bring down to the ground a player who has the ball. Also, a position on both the offensive and defensive line.

tight end   An offensive player who lines up on the line of scrimmage next to the offensive tackle and is used as either a blocker or a receiver.

touchdown   A six-point play in which any part of the ball crosses the plane of the opponent's goal line while in the possession of an inbounds player.

turnover   A change of ball possession because of a recovered fumble or interception.

two-point conversion   A two-point scoring play after a touch-down from the two-yard line during which a team success-fully runs or passes the ball into the opponent's end zone.

yardage   Distance gained or lost during a play from the line of scrimmage.

BIBLIOGRAPHY

Bofah, Kofi. "The Greatest NFL Running Backs of All Time." Associated Content, April 30, 2009. Available online. URL: http://www.associatedcontent.com/article/1697416/the_ greatest_nfl_running_backs_of_all.html?cat=14.

Craig, Mark. "New Viking Carries Heartache; Tragedy Has Been a Frequent Visitor in Adrian Peterson's Life." *Minneapolis Star Tribune*, April 30, 2007.

Currie, Stephen. *Adrian Peterson.* Broomall, Pa.: Mason Crest Publishers, 2009.

D'Alessio, Jeff. "My Profile: Vikings Pro Bowl RB Adrian Peterson." *Sporting News*, August 31, 2009. Available online. URL: http://aol.sportingnews.com/nfl/story/2009-08-31/my-profile-vikings-pro-bowl-rb-adrian-peterson?developing-stories-sport-NFL=NCAAF.

Evans, Thayer. "Red River Reunion." *New York Times*, August 27, 2006.

———. "The Pride of Palestine: Texas Town Follows Its Star." *New York Times*, September 23, 2007.

Freeman, Mike. *Bloody Sundays: Inside the Dazzling, Rough-and-Tumble World of the NFL.* New York: HarperCollins, 2003.

Gay, Timothy. *The Physics of Football: Discover the Science of Bone-Crunching Hits, Soaring Field Goals, and Awe-Inspiring Passes.* New York: HarperCollins, 2004.

Greenberg, Steve. "Sporting News Conversation: Jim Brown Interviews Adrian Peterson." *Sporting News*, August 3, 2009.

Hoover, John. "Bad Breaks Follow A.D.: Adrian Peterson's Mom, Bonita Jackson, Broke Her Leg Saturday." *Tulsa World*, October 17, 2006.

———. "Big Dreams: Adrian Peterson: Athletic Destiny." *Tulsa World*, August 20, 2008.

———. "Sight for Sore Eyes: Nelson Peterson Finally Gets the Chance to See His Son Adrian Play College Football in Person Saturday." *Tulsa World*, October 11, 2006.

Isaacson, Melissa. "OU's Peterson Overcomes Family Strife to Show National Promise." *Chicago Tribune*, October 29, 2004.

King, Peter. "Training Camp Postcard: Vikings." SI.com, August 8, 2007. Available online. URL: http://sportsillustrated.cnn.com/2007/writers/peter_king/08/08/vikings.postcard/.

Latzke, Jeff. "Now Free, Peterson's Dad to See Him Play." Associated Press, October 13, 2006.

Lewis, Michael. *The Blind Side.* New York: W.W. Norton, 2006.

NBC Sports. "Top 10 Running Backs of All Time." NBCSports.com, February 6, 2005. Available online. URL: http://nbcsports.msnbc.com/id/6907909.

Scoggins, Chip. "A Return to Form in More Ways Than One." *Minneapolis Star Tribune*, January 25, 2010.

———. "History Lesson: As Adrian Peterson Heads Toward the NFL Rushing Title in His Second Season, Many of the All-Time Greats Already Have Called the Second-year Viking the League's Best Running Back." *Minneapolis Star Tribune*, December 14, 2008.

———. "Vikings Training Camp; Peterson Is Confident He's Elevated His Game." *Minneapolis Star Tribune*, August 3, 2008.

Seifert, Kevin. "Adrian Peterson Works on Grasp." ESPN.com, September 6, 2010. Available online. URL: http://sports.espn.go.com/nfl/news/story?id=5540032.

———. "Fine-tuning a Talent: Adrian Peterson's Skills Are Stunning Enough, But His Ability to Take Direction and Set Up His Blockers Made Him a Record-setter." *Minneapolis Star Tribune*, November 6, 2007.

———. "Setting Up the Big Play." ESPN.com, November 11, 2008. Available online. URL: http://espn.go.com/blog/nfc-north/post/_/id/871/setting-up-the-big-play.

———. "Vikings Rookie Feels Right at Home." *Minneapolis Star Tribune*, November 4, 2007.

Sexton, Sally. "'God Kept Me Focused.'" *Palestine Herald-Press*, June 22, 2008.

Souhan, Jim. "Like Mother, Like Son: If You Think Adrian's Fast, You Should See His Mother." *Minneapolis Star Tribune*, November 13, 2008.

Stuart, Chase. "Best Running Backs." Pro-Football Reference, August 3, 2009. Available online. URL: http://www.pro-football-reference.com.

Tyler, Scott. "Offering a Helping Hand." *Palestine Herald-Press*, June 14, 2009.

Wojciechowski, Gene. "Next Athlete: Adrian Peterson." *ESPN Magazine*, October 15, 2008. Available online. URL: http://sports.espn.go.com/espnmag/story?section=magazine&id=3645380.

Wuebben, Joe. "Run, Adrian, Run." *Muscle & Fitness*, October 2008.

Zulgad, Judd. "Getting to Know You." *Minneapolis Star Tribune*, February 20, 2008.

———. "Vikings Insider; Peterson Will to Win Is Making the Vikings 'His Team.'" *Minneapolis Star Tribune*, November 16, 2008.

———. "Vikings 2007; Adrian Peterson: Sublime, Yes, But Also Subtle." *Minneapolis Star Tribune*, September 7, 2007.

FURTHER READING

Athlon Sports. *Sooner Pride: Oklahoma Spirit Shines Through an Unforgettable Season.* Chicago, Il.: Triumph Books, 2005.

Dunn, Warrick, and Don Yeager. *Running for My Life: My Journey in the Game of Football and Beyond.* New York: HarperCollins, 2008.

Hack, Damon. "The Virtue of Patience." *Sports Illustrated,* October 15, 2007.

MacCambridge, Michael. *America's Game: The Epic Story of How Pro Football Captured a Nation.* New York: Random House, 2004.

Maske, Mark. *War Without Death: A Year of Extreme Competition in Pro Football's NFC East.* New York: Penguin Press, 2007.

WEB SITES

Adrian Peterson (a fan site)
http://www.adrian-peterson.com

Adrian Peterson Online (a fan site)
http://www.adrianpetersononline.com

Minnesota Vikings
http://www.vikings.com

NFL
http://www.nfl.com

Purple Pride: Home of Vikings Fans Worldwide
http://www.purplepride.org

PICTURE CREDITS

INDEX

50 Cent, 70

A

Adrian Peterson (Currie), 45–46
Adrian Peterson Day, 70–72, 84
Adrian Peterson Football Camp, 70, 85
AFC. *See* American Football Conference
All-American honors, 28–29
All Day Foundation, 70, 84
All-USA High School Football Team, 28
American Football Conference (AFC), 67–68
Anderson County Youth Football League, 20–21
Andrews, Shawn, 68
Arizona Cardinals, 76, 96
Associated Press
   interviews, 13, 22, 45, 51, 63, 65, 77, 83, 85
Associated Press NFL Offensive Rookie of the Year, 65–66
Atlanta Falcons
   games against, 57–58, 77, 79

B

Barrett, David, 57
Berrian, Bernard, 74, 76, 80, 85
Berry, Halle, 63
Bert Bell Award, 82
Bieniemy, Eric
   coach, 54, 57, 72, 86
Bigby, Atari, 13
Birk, Matt, 58
Blind Side, The (Lewis), 29
Bloody Sundays (Freeman), 66, 91
Boise State University, 47–48
Bollinger, Brooks, 61
Bowling Green University, 35
Boys and Girls Club, 77
Brees, Drew, 82

Brown, Guy, 71
Brown, Jim, 65, 90–92
   interview with, 88–89
Brown, Mack, 37
Bryant, Bear, 29
Bryant, Kobe, 63
Bush, Reggie, 40–41, 69

C

Campbell, Dave, 63
Campbell, Earl, 80, 89–90
charity donations, 70
Chicago Bears
   games against, 58–60, 65, 76
Chicago Tribune, 23
childhood
   family, 16–17, 19, 21–22
   and football, 19–32
   and track, 22–23, 28
Childress, Brad
   coach, 13, 15, 52, 73–76, 79, 87, 97
Cimarron (Ferber), 36
Cincinnati Bengals, 12
Cleveland Browns, 12, 51–52, 92
Cook, Ryan, 11
Cotton Bowl, 36
Craig, Mark, 21, 53
Cruise, Tom, 36
Currie, Stephen, 55
   Adrian Peterson, 45–46

D

D'Alessio, Jeff, 63
Dallas Cowboys, 12, 71, 93
   fan, 19–21
Dallas, Texas, 17, 36
Dawkins, Brian, 80
Denver Broncos, 65
Detroit Lions, 65, 76, 92, 96
Dickerson, Eric
   career, 25–28, 65, 77, 80, 90–91
Dogra, Ben, 52–53

Dorsett, Tony, 90
Dyson, Andre, 57

E

East Texas Food Bank, 70
Eden Prairie, Minnesota, 52
  living in, 56, 63–64
education, 19–20, 22
  college, 32–51, 88
  high school, 23–32
Elway, John, 27
endorsements
  commercials, 70, 84, 97
  contracts, 52
ESPN
  coverage, 28, 31, 33, 39–40,
    47, 52, 60, 63, 76, 96–97
ESPN.com, 15, 70, 73
Eudey, Steve
  mentor, 17, 20, 23
Evans, Thayer
  interviews, 19, 21, 28–29, 44,
    55–56

F

Far and Away (movie), 36
Faulk, Marshall, 67–68, 90, 93
Favre, Brett
  teammate, 85, 88, 92–94, 96
Feed the Children, 84
Ferber, Edna
  Cimarron, 36
Fiesta Bowl, 47–48, 50, 65
Foxx, Jamie, 63
Freeman, Mike, 90
  Bloody Sundays, 66, 91
Frerotte, Gus
  teammate, 11, 74, 76, 79

G

Gay, Timothy
  The Physics of Football, 78
Goodell, Roger, 52
Green Bay Packers, 85

fans, 8
games against, 8, 10–11, 13,
    15, 58, 64, 73–74, 93, 96
rivalries, 7, 10–12, 64, 73, 93
Greenberg, Steve, 13, 15, 88
Gruden, Jon, 93

H

Hall, DeAngelo, 58
Harrell, Jeff
  coach, 23–25, 28
Harris, Al, 64
Harvin, Percy
  teammate, 86, 92–93
Heisman Trophy
  candidate, 39–40
  winners, 34, 40, 45
Herrera, Anthony, 11
Hoover, John
  interviews, 17, 20, 31, 41, 46
Houston Texans, 88
Howard, Dwight, 70
Hutchinson, Steve, 92

I

Idaho State University, 17
Indianapolis Colts, 82
  games against, 73
injuries, 8, 51, 53, 66, 72
  ankles, 42–43, 64, 96
  collarbone fracture, 46–47, 50
  dislocated shoulder, 40–41, 64
  hamstring, 74
  knees, 64–65, 67, 69
Iowa State University, 45–46
Irvin, Michael, 19
Isaacson, Melissa, 23, 28, 34, 38

J

Jackson, Bonita Brown (mother),
  46
  support of, 10, 19, 22–23, 33,
    53, 64, 72
  track star, 16–17, 22–23

Jackson, Frankie (stepfather), 21, 53
  support of, 10
Jackson, Tarvaris
  teammate, 57, 61, 70, 74, 79–80
Jacksonville Jaguars, 75
Jacobs, Brandon, 89
James, Edgerrin, 80, 90
James, LeBron, 63
Jaworski, Ron, 93
Jeter, Derek, 43
Jones-Drew, Maurice, 89
Jones, Kejuan, 34–35
Jordon, Michael, 43

K

Kansas State University, 39, 43
Kidman, Nicole, 36
King, Domanique, 28
King, Peter, 55, 75
Kleinsasser, Jim, 61
Krawczynski, Jon, 13

L

Latzke, Jeff, 45, 51
Leinart, Matt, 40–41
Lemming, Tom, 28–29
Lewis, Jamal, 62
Lewis, Michael
  The Blind Side, 29
Li'l Wayne, 63
Long, Chuck, 34
Longwell, Ryan, 60, 79
Los Angeles, 69
Los Angeles Rams, 26
Louisiana State University, 31

M

Manning, Peyton, 82
Martin, Curtis, 90
Matson, Ollie, 89
Matthews, Clay, 93
Matthews, Dave, 94

Maxwell Football Club, 82
McCoy, Colt, 45
McKinnie, Bryant, 56
McNabb, Donovan, 81
media
  attention, 73, 79, 82, 84, 86
Miami Dolphins, 96
Minneapolis-Star-Tribune
  interviews in, 13, 21–22, 55, 63, 67, 72
Minnesota State University, 54
Minnesota Vikings
  coaches, 9, 13–15, 52, 54–55, 57, 61, 70, 72–76, 79, 86–88, 97
  contracts with, 53–54
  fans, 8, 10–11, 15, 56–57, 66, 73, 80, 82, 87
  gjallarhorn, 11
  history, 76, 80
  mascot, 11
  Metrodome, 10–11, 13, 57, 60, 73–74, 77, 79–80, 93, 96
  playing for, 52–98
  play-offs, 65, 80–82, 93
  rivalries, 7, 10–13, 64, 73, 93
  rookie year, 8, 54–68, 86
  teammates, 11, 13–15, 55–58, 60–61, 68, 70, 72, 74, 76, 79–80, 82, 85–86, 88, 92–94, 96
  training camps, 54–56, 65, 72–73, 86–87
M.O.M. (Mothers on a Mission) Squad, 70
Monday Night Football, 73, 93

N

National Basketball Association (NBA), 17
National Football Conference (NFC), 7, 67–68, 73, 76, 83
  championship game, 77, 79, 93–94

National Football League (NFL),
7, 11, 21, 25, 77–78
  drafts, 27, 29, 41, 46–47,
  49–53, 57, 85
  fans, 8, 52, 85
  films, 85
  Hall of Fame, 63
  history, 60, 62, 80, 82, 91, 94
  MVP, 73, 82
  play-offs, 8, 80, 93
  records, 62–64
  scouts, 41, 50–51
  tryouts, 10
National Invitational Camp,
50–51
NBA. *See* National Basketball
Association
NCAA rules, 44
New England, Patriots, 12
New Orleans Saints, 69, 74, 82,
93–94
Newton's Second Law of Motion,
78
New York Giants, 12
  games against, 79
New York Jets, 12, 57, 85
New York Times, 56
NFC. *See* National Football
Conference
NFL. See National Football
League
NFL Network, 52, 60, 63
Notorious B.I.G., 63

O

Oklahoma State University, 39,
43
Orange Bowl, 40–41
Organized Team Activity, 86
Ortiz, David, 70
Owens, Terrell, 64

P

Palestine Herald-Press, 70

Palestine High School, 53
  football at, 23–25
Palestine, Texas, 63, 70–71, 84
  growing up in, 16–32, 51, 57,
  97
  parade in, 53
Paris, Chris (stepbrother)
  murder of, 10, 51
Parker, De'Mond, 39
Paul Bunyan's Axe trophy, 7
Payton, Walter, 90–91
Peterson, Ade'ja (daughter),
44, 56
Peterson, Brian (brother), 33
  death, 10, 17, 19, 21, 23
Peterson, Derrick (half-brother),
56, 63
Peterson, Nelson (father)
  and football, 17, 19–20, 38,
  41
  gunshot wound, 17
  incarceration, 10, 21–23, 29,
  31, 35
  relationship with, 21–22
  release from prison, 45
  support of, 10, 20, 25–26, 29,
  31, 39, 45–46, 53, 56, 82
Philadelphia Eagles, 12
  games against, 80–82, 96
Physics of Football, The (Gay),
78
Pitt, Brad, 94
Pittsburgh Steelers, 12
Portis, Clinton, 80
Pro Bowl, 66, 82–83, 91, 93
  MVP, 67–68

Q

quarterbacks, 25, 31, 41, 51, 61,
70, 74
  famous, 24, 27, 34, 52, 79,
  81–82, 85, 93–94
  inexperienced, 57–58, 96
  protection, 55

R

Red River Showdown
 games, 12, 35–39, 43, 45
Richardson, Tony, 55
Romo, Tony, 93
running back/tailbacks, 19, 24,
 52
 best, 29, 40, 77, 79, 88–92, 98
 carries, 26–27, 35, 39, 41–42,
  49, 57–58, 65, 74, 76, 83,
  92–93
 fling, 37
 fumbles, 13, 77, 79, 86
 hits, 75, 80, 97
 job description, 11, 13–14, 51,
  55, 97
 quickness, 8–9, 20, 25, 57, 92
 records, 8, 39, 60, 62–63, 76
 rushing, 8, 39, 76, 79
 skill development, 10, 31, 50,
  52, 55, 61, 66–67, 69, 72,
  77–78, 86–87
 speed, 8–9, 20, 25, 27, 39, 51,
  60–61, 88, 91–92
 touchdowns, 13, 15, 26–27,
  32, 35, 41–47, 49, 58, 60–61,
  65, 68, 75, 79–80, 82–83, 88,
  92–94, 96
 vision, 28, 89–92
Russell, JaMarcus, 52

S

Salter, Carolyn, 71
Samuel, Assante, 80
Sanders, Barry, 90–91
Sanders, Deion, 19
San Diego Chargers
 games against, 8, 60–61
San Francisco 49ers
 games against, 65
Savage, Phil, 51
Sayers, Gale, 89–91
Schembechler, Bo, 29

Schmidt, Jerry, 33–34
Scoggins, Chip
 interviews, 69, 72–73, 76–77,
  86, 94
Seifert, Kevin
 interviews, 15, 56, 63–64, 86,
  96–97
Sexton, Sally, 70
Sharper, Darren, 72
Simpson, Ashlee, 41
Simpson, O.J., 90
Sims, Billy, 49
Smith, Alex, 40
Smith, Emmitt, 43, 65–66, 77,
 90–91
SMU. *See* Southern Methodist
 University
Souhan, Jim, 22, 67
Southern Methodist University
 (SMU), 26
Special Olympics, 70
Sporting News, 13, 15, 63, 88
Sports Center, 31
sports rivalries, 12, 35
Star Tribune, 53, 69
St. Louis Rams, 56
Stoops, Bob
 coach, 29, 46–47
Super Bowl, 8, 73, 76, 82, 94
Swift, Taylor, 94

T

Tampa Bay Buccaneers,
 74–75
Taylor, Chester, 57–58
Texarkana tournament, 20–21
Texas, 15
 football in, 25–28, 70
Texas A&M University, 39–40
Texas Christian University, 42
Texas Tech University, 35
Thomas, Thurman, 90
Tillman, Charles, 60
Tirico, Mike, 93

Tomlinson, LaDainian, 60, 65, 77, 89–90
track star, 22–24
Tulsa World, 17
Tyler, Scott, 85

U

University of Alabama at Birmingham, 29, 44
University of Florida, 86
University of Houston, 17, 35
University of Minnesota, 7
University of Oklahoma, 12
   coaches, 29, 33–34, 37, 46–47
   conditioning program, 33–34
   controversy at, 43–44
   fans, 35–36, 41, 43, 46
   football at, 24, 26, 29, 31–49, 51, 88
   national championships, 40
   playing for, 33–49, 51
   Pro day at, 51
   teammates, 34–35, 37, 40, 42–44, 46–47, 51
University of Oregon, 35, 44–45
University of Southern California, 31, 40–41
University of Texas, 12, 31
   fans, 35–36
   games against, 31, 35–39, 45
University of Tulsa, 42

University of Utah, 40
University of Washington, 44
University of Wisconsin, 7
U.S. Army All-American Bowl, 31–32
U.S. Army National Player of the Year, 32
USA Today, 28, 51
U.S. Olympic team, 17

W

Washington, Joe, 49
Washington Redskins, 12, 65
Webb, Joe, 96
Westbrook, Brian, 82
Westwood Junior High, 22–23
White, Jason
   teammate, 34–35, 40
wide receiver, 51
Williams, Ricky, 67
Wilner, Barry, 65
Wojciechowski, Gene, 31, 33, 39, 41
Woods, Tiger, 63
World War II, 31
Wuebben, Joe, 16

Z

Zulgad, Judd, 13, 55–57, 74

ABOUT THE AUTHOR

CLIFFORD W. MILLS is an adjunct faculty member at Columbia College, an editor, and a writer who specializes in biographies of world leaders and sports figures. He is a lifelong football fan who lives in Jacksonville, Florida, and roots for both the home team and the New England Patriots.